AN ENEMY
CALLED AVERAGE

by
John L. Mason

Honor Books
Tulsa, Oklahoma

An Enemy Called Average
ISBN 1-56292-046-4
Copyright © 1993 by John Mason
P.O. Box 54996
Tulsa, OK 74155

FOREWORD

Some years ago, a researcher decided to find the secret of success. After months of study and countless interviews, he finally gave up. "There is not a secret," he said, "it is all related to hard work. One must climb the ladder to success, not just be lifted on an elevator." The successful individual is the one who will do what the average person will not do. And average is nothing more than being the top of the bottom.

Thinking wrong, believing wrong, and confessing wrong always leads to an unhappy, mediocre and unprofitable way of life.

To think success, to become better, to believe big and to strive to be above average, you must develop the right kind of mental processes. You have been programmed to be negative, to disbelieve, to be skeptical. However, you can change. That negative experience, the minuses — these can be transformed into positives and pluses simply by changing your attitudes.

William James said, "The greatest discovery of my generation is that men can change their circumstances by changing their attitude of mind." We teach changing those thoughts by changing the input. What goes in must come out.

Some say success is just a decision away. That is true, on the surface. But that decision must be backed up with solid effort.

A person with a winning attitude accounts for 80 percent of the results in this country today. It's amazing that the figures don't change from year to year. They stay about the same. Twenty percent of the people are getting 80 percent of the results and 80 percent of the people are getting 20% of the results. That isn't very much when you realize these figures haven't changed over the last 25 years.

Your growth potential, return on your investment, rewards in proportion to your efforts, and personal independence are limited only by your vision and desire. This already has made you above average. So be enthusiastic! You have a lot to be excited about. God created you in the likeness of Himself and endowed you with specific talents and abilities. As you develop those areas in your life and use them to help others, you won't have to be concerned about being above average. You will have conquered that enemy.

Dexter R. Yager, Sr.

DEDICATION

I am proud to dedicate this book to my beautiful wife, Linda, and our four wonderful children, Michelle, Greg, Mike, and David.

To Linda, for her steadfastness and love;

To Michelle, for her creativity and enthusiasm;

To Greg, for his patient perseverance and willingness to help;

To Mike, who through his little boy love for me reminds me how we are to love the Father.

To David, who, by his happiness, always keeps my perspective accurate.

Without their support, help, encouragement, sense of humor, and prayers, this book would still be sitting in the various and sundry files from whence it came.

CONTENTS

ACKNOWLEDGMENTS

It is impossible to write a book like this one without the help of "foundational-level" people. Special thanks to:

Billy Joe Daugherty, whose messages have consistently inspired me to bound past mediocrity;

Roberts Liardon, who challenged me to walk in the Spirit and not live another day in neutral;

Keith Provance, the best example of a leader I have ever known;

Mike Loomis, who always offers a timely word of encouragement;

Tim Redmond, whose insight and advice has been invaluable;

Tom Winters, whose integrity and character inspires me.

INTRODUCTION

Mediocrity is a region bounded on the north by compromise, on the south by indecision, on the east by past thinking, and on the west by a lack of vision.

One morning as I woke up, the first thought that came to my mind before my feet hit the floor was the phrase "An Enemy Called Average." At that moment I knew that God had given me the title for the book which had been stirring within me for so long.

The purpose of this book is to address areas in your life that need improvement and to stir up the God-given gifts and call within you. Every person has been endowed with a certain mixture of abilities and opportunities which makes him unique. No mixture is insignificant. There is something that God has placed within each of us that causes us to cry out to be above average and extraordinary.

I felt led to write this book in a "nugget" style in order to deliver as much meat as possible in an enjoyable, easy-to-read format. In Genesis, chapter three, verse nine, God asked Adam, "Where are you?" He is still asking that question of each of us today. Where are we in regard to God's plan for our lives? Where are we concerning the gifts and talents He has given us?

It is my prayer that as you read this book, you will allow the Holy Spirit to reveal God's plan for you and to inform, exhort, and correct you so that you will bound past every area of mediocrity and find total fulfillment in your life.

PART I:
LOOKING INWARD

NUGGET #1

From This Page You Can Go Anywhere You Want To

Do you know what this page is noted for? This page can be the springboard to your future. You can start here and go anywhere you want to.

God has placed within each of us the potential and opportunity for success. Yet, it takes just as much effort to lead a bad life as it does a good life. Still, millions lead aimless lives in prisons of their own making — simply because they haven't decided what to do with their lives. A lot of people confuse bad decision-making with destiny (Kin Hubbard). "*Where there is no vision, the people perish,*" says Proverbs 29:18. That's not God's plan for you. Dissatisfaction is not the absence of things but the absence of vision. It always costs more not to do God's will than to do it.

When you are an original and know God's plan, you shine like the stars of the firmament. Copies are like the darkness in which they float. You can predict a person's future by his awareness of his destiny. Life's heaviest burden is to have nothing to carry. The significance of any person is determined by the cause for which he lives and the price he is willing to pay. **What you set your heart on will determine how you spend your life.**

Do not take lightly the dreams and hopes God has given for your life. Cherish them, for they are like children birthed within you. "It is better to die for something than it is to live for nothing," says Dr. Bob Jones, Sr. A man without principle never draws much interest.

No wind blows in favor of a ship without a destination. A person without a conviction is like a ship without a rudder. People generally have too many opinions and not enough convictions. **God plants no yearning in you that He does not intend to satisfy.** We all distrust our hearts too much and our heads not enough. As long as God's direction is your friend, don't worry about your enemies. It is not the man with a motive but the man with a purpose who prevails. "Every man's destiny is his life preserver" (The Sunday School).

NUGGET #2

Beige Should Be Your Least Favorite Color

Never try to defend your present position and situation. Choose to be a person who is on the offensive, not the defensive. **People who live defensively never rise above being average.** We're called, as Christians, to be on the offensive, to take the initiative. A lukewarm, indecisive person is never secure regardless of his wealth, education, or position.

Don't ever let your quest for balance become an excuse for not taking the unique, radical, invading move that God has directed you to take. Many times the attempt to maintain balance in life is really just an excuse for being lukewarm. In Joshua 1:6,7,9 the Lord says three times to Joshua, *"Be strong and courageous."* I believe that He is saying the same thing to all believers today.

When you choose to be on the offensive, the atmosphere of your life will begin to change. So if you don't like the atmosphere of your life, choose to take the offensive position. Taking the offensive is not just an action taken outside a person; it is always a decision made within.

When you do choose to be on the offensive, keep all your conflicts impersonal. Fight the issue, not the person. Speak about what God in you can do, not what others cannot do. **You will find that when all of your reasons are defensive, your cause almost never succeeds.**

Being on the offensive and taking the initiative is a master key which opens the door to opportunity in your life. Learn to create a habit of taking the initiative and **don't ever start your day in neutral.** Every morning when your feet hit the floor, you should be thinking on the offensive, reacting like an invader, taking control of your day and your life.

By pulling back and being defensive usually you enhance the problem. Intimidation always precedes defeat. If you are not sure which way to go, pray and move towards the situation in confident trust.

Be like the two fishermen who got trapped in a storm in the middle of the lake. One turned to the other and asked, "Should we pray, or should we row?" His wise companion responded, "Let's do both!"

That's taking the offensive.

NUGGET #3

Growth Comes From Building on Talents, Gifts, and Strengths – Not by Solving Problems

One of the most neglected areas in many people's lives is the area of gifts that God has placed within them. It is amazing how some people can devote their entire lives to a field of endeavor or a profession that has nothing to do with their inborn talents. In fact, the opposite is also true. Many people spend their whole lifetime trying to change who God has made them to be. They ignore their God-given talents while continually seeking to change their natural makeup. As children of God, we need to recognize our innate gifts, talents, and strengths and do everything in our power to build on them.

One good thing about God's gifts and calling is that they are permanent and enduring. Romans 11:29 tells us: *...the gifts and calling of God are without re-pentance.* The Greek word translated *repentance* in this verse means "irrevocable." God cannot take away His gifts and calling in your life. Even if you've never done anything with them, even if you've failed time and time again, God's gifts and calling are still resident within you. They are there this day, and you can choose to do something with them, beginning right now.

Gifts and talents are really God's deposits in our personal accounts, but we determine the interest onthem. The greater the amount of interest and attention we give to them, the greater their value becomes. God's gifts are never loans; they are always deposits. As such, they are never used up or depleted. In fact, the more they are used, the greater, stronger, and more valuable they become. When they are put to good use, they provide information, insight, and revelation which cannot be received any other way or from any other source.

As Christians, we need to make full use of all the gifts and talents which God has bestowed upon us so that we do not abound in one area while becoming bankrupt in another. Someone has said, "If the only tool you have is a hammer, you tend to treat everything like a nail." Don't make that mistake; use all of the gifts God has given you. If you choose not to step out and make maximum use of the gifts and talents in your life, you will spend your days on this earth helping someone else reach his goals. Most people let others control their destiny. Don't allow anyone to take over the driver's seat in your life. Fulfill your own dreams and determine your own life's course.

Never underestimate the power of the gifts that are within you. **Gifts and talents are given us to use not only so we can fulfill to the fullest the call in our own lives, but also so we can reach the souls who are attached to those gifts.** There are people whose lives are waiting to be affected by what God has placed within you. So evaluate yourself. Define and refine your gifts, talents and strengths. Choose today to look for opportunities to exercise your unique God-endowed, God-ordained gifts and calling.

NUGGET #4

"The Nose of the Bulldog is Slanted Backwards So He Can Continue To Breathe Without Letting Go"
– WINSTON CHURCHILL

Persistent people begin their success where most others quit. We Christians need to be known as people of persistence and endurance. **One person with commitment, persistence, and endurance will accomplish more than a thousand people with interest alone.** In Hebrews 12:1 (NIV) we read: *Therefore, since we are surrounded by such a great cloud of witnesses, let us throw off everything that hinders and the sin that so easily entangles, and let us run with perseverance the race marked out for us.* The more diligently we work, the harder it is to quit. Persistence is a habit; so is quitting.

Never worry about how much money, ability, or equipment you are starting with. Just begin with a million dollars worth of determination. Remember: **it's not what you have, it's what you do with what you have that makes all the difference.** Many people eagerly begin "the good fight of faith," but they forget to add patience, persistence, and endurance to their enthusiasm. Josh Billings said, "Consider the postage stamp. Its usefulness consists in the ability to stick to something until it gets there." You and I should be known as "postage-stamp" Christians.

In First Corinthians 15:58, the Apostle Paul writes: *Therefore, my beloved brethren, be ye stedfast,unmoveable, always abounding in the work of the Lord, forasmuch as ye know that your labour is not in vain*

in the Lord. Peter tells us: *Wherefore, beloved, seeing that ye look for such things, be diligent that ye may be found of him in peace, without spot, and blameless* (2 Pet. 3:14). And wise Solomon points out: *Seest thou a man diligent in his business? he shall stand before kings...*(Prov. 22:29). In the Far East the people plant a tree called the Chinese bamboo. During the first four years they water and fertilize the plant with seemingly little or no results. Then the fifth year they again apply water and fertilizer — and in five weeks' time the tree grows ninety feet in height! The obvious question is: did the Chinese bamboo tree grow ninety feet in five weeks, or did it grow ninety feet in five years? The answer is: it grew ninety feet in five years. Because if at any time during those five years the people had stopped watering and fertilizing the tree, it would have died.

Many times our dreams and plans appear not to be succeeding. We are tempted to give up and quit trying. Instead, we need to continue to water and fertilize those dreams and plans, nurturing the seeds of the vision God has placed within us. Because we know that if we do not quit, if we display perseverance and endurance, we will also reap a harvest. Charles Haddon Spurgeon said, "By perseverance the snail reached the ark." We need to be like that snail.

NUGGET #5

How Many Outstanding Generalities Do You Know?

How many outstanding people do you know with unique and distinctive characteristics? Don't be a living custard. It's true what Eric Hoffer said: "When people are free to do as they please, they usually imitate each other." **Man is the only creation who refuses to be what he is.**

Don't just look for miracles. You are a miracle. You are *"fearfully and wonderfully made"* (Ps. 139:14). Do not be awestruck by other people and try to copy them. Nobody can be you as efficiently and as effectively as you can. One of the hardest things about climbing the ladder of success is getting through the crowd of copies at the bottom. The number of people who don't take advantage of their talents is more than made up for by the number who take advantage of the talents they scarcely have.

You are a specialist. You are not created to be all things to all people. More than 90 percent of all flowers have either an unpleasant odor or none at all. Yet, it is the ones with sweet fragrance that we most remember. Stand out! "Following the path of least resistance is what makes men and rivers crooked," says Larry Bielat. Too many people make cemeteries of their lives by burying their talents and gifts.

The copy adapts himself to the world, but the original tries to adapt the world to him. *"Don't copy the behaviors and customs of this world, but be a new and different person with*

a fresh newness in all you do and think. Then you will learn from your own experience how his ways will really satisfy you" (Rom. 12:2, TLB).

It doesn't take a majority to make a change — it takes only a few determined originals and a sound cause. You're the only one in all of creation who has your set of abilities. You're special...you're rare. And in all rarity there is great worth. You are not insignificant; you are valuable and precious. God loves you just the way you are, but He loves you too much to leave you the way you are.

"Could Hamlet have been written by a committee, or the Mona Lisa painted by a club? Could the New Testament have been composed as a conference report? Creative ideas do not spring from groups. They spring from individuals. The divine spark leaps from the finger of God to the finger of Adam," said A. Whitney Griswold.

While an original is always hard to find, he is easy to recognize. God leads every soul in an individual way. There are no precedents: You are the first You that ever was. Being a minority in itself never makes you right. Being right always makes you a minority. *"Wide is the gate, and broad is the way, that leadeth to destruction,"* said Jesus in Matthew 7:13. There is not enough darkness in the whole world to put out the light that God has put in you.

NUGGET #6

You're Like a Teabag – Not Worth Much Till You've Been Through Some Hot Water

Have you ever failed or made a mistake? Good, then this nugget is for you. **The fact that you've failed is proof that you're not finished.** Failures and mistakes can be a bridge, not a barricade, to success.

Psalm 37:23,24 says, "*The steps of a good man are ordered by the Lord: and he delighteth in his way. Though he fall, he shall not be utterly cast down: for the Lord upholdeth him with his hand.*" Failure may look like a fact, but it's just an opinion. Successful people believe that mistakes are just feedback. It's not how far you fall but how high you bounce that makes all the difference.

Theodore Roosevelt said, "Far better it is to dare mighty things, to win glorious triumphs, even though checkered by failure than to rank with those poor spirits who neither enjoy much nor suffer much because they live in the great twilight that knows not victory or defeat." One of the riskiest things you can do in life is to take too many precautions and never have any failures or mistakes. Failure is the opportunity to start over more intelligently.

No one ever achieved worthwhile success who did not, at one time or another, teeter on the edge of disaster. If you have tried to do something and failed, you are vastly better off than if you had tried to do nothing and succeeded. **The person who never makes a mistake must get awfully tired doing nothing.** If you're not making mistakes, you're not risking enough.

31

Vernon Sanders says, "Experience is a hard teacher because she gives the test first, the lesson afterwards." Experience is what you get when you are looking for something else. But the experience of failure always makes you either better or bitter. The choice is up to you. The good news is that God has no plans that end in failure. Jeremiah 29:11 (NIV) says, "'*For I know the plans I have for you,' declares the Lord, 'plans to prosper you and not to harm you, plans to give you hope and a future.'*"

Success consists of getting up just one time more than you fell down. "You don't drown by falling in the water; you drown by staying there," said author Edwin Louis Cole. So get up and go on. Proverbs 28:13 (TLB) says, "*A man who refuses to admit his mistakes can never be successful. But if he confesses and forsakes them, he gets another chance.*"

The death of your dream will not be accomplished by a major failure. Its death will come from indifference and apathy. The best way to go on after a failure is to learn the lesson and forget the details. If you don't, you'll become like the scalded dog that fears hot water, and afterwards cold.

Failure can become a weight or it can give you wings. The only way to make a comeback is to go on. **If the truth were known, 99 percent of success is built on former failure.** A mistake proves somebody stopped talking long enough to do something.

Remember the old poem that says, "Success is failure turned inside out, the silver tint of the clouds of doubt, and you never can tell how close you are, it may be near when it seems so far. So stick to the fight when you're hardest hit, it's when things seem worse that you must not quit" (Unknown).

NUGGET #7

Failure is Waiting on the Path of Least Persistence

Never give up on what you know you really should do. The person with big dreams is more powerful than the person with all the facts. Remember, overnight success takes about ten years. The "man of the hour" spent many days and nights getting there. Consider the man who said, "My overnight success was the longest night of my life." Winners simply do what losers don't want to do.

Earl Nightingale said, "A young man once asked a great and famous older man, 'How can I make a name for myself in the world and become successful?' The great and famous man replied: 'You have only to decide upon what it is you want and then stay with it, never deviating from your course no matter how long it takes, or how rough the road, until you have accomplished it.'" **Success is largely a matter of holding on after others have let go.**

In the confrontation between the stream and the rock, the stream always wins — not through strength but through perseverance. Christopher Morley said, "Big shots are only little shots that keep shooting." Persistence is simply enjoying the distance between the fulfillment of God's promises.

Judas was an example of someone who started the good fight of faith but lacked persistence. God wants us to be people of strong wills, not strong won'ts. Many of the world's great failures did not realize how close they were to success when they gave up. Stopping at third base adds no more score than striking out. We rate success by what people finish, not by what they start. People do not fail, they just quit too easily. **God won't give up on you! Don't you give up on God!** *"For I am persuaded that neither death, nor life, nor angels, nor principalities, nor powers, nor things present, nor things to come, nor height, nor depth, nor any other creature, shall be able to separate us from the love of God, which is in Christ Jesus our Lord"* (Rom. 8:38,39).

Your persistence is proof you have not yet been defeated. Mike Murdock says, "You have no right to anything you have not pursued. For the proof of desire is in the pursuit." So, *"Commit to the Lord whatever you do, and your plans will succeed."* (Prov. 16:3, NIV). Life holds no greater wealth than that of steadfast commitment. It cannot be robbed from you. Only you can lose it by your will.

The destiny of the diligent is to stand in the company of leaders. *"Seest thou a man diligent in his business? he shall stand before kings"* (Prov. 22:29). **When faithfulness is most difficult, it is most necessary, because trying times are no time to quit trying.** The secret of success is to start from scratch and keep on scratching.

NUGGET #8

Passion Is The Spark
for Your Fuse

God has put inside every person the potential to be passionate. One person with passion is greater than the passive force of ninety-nine who have only an interest. Too many people have "only an interest" in their destiny. The book of Ecclesiastes says, "*Whatsoever thy hand findeth to do, do it with thy might*" (9:10).

Everyone loves something. We are shaped and motivated by what we love. It is our passion. **Ignore what you are passionate about, and you ignore one of the greatest potentials that God has put inside you.** Nothing significant was ever achieved without passion. Jesus was a passionate man. He died for us because He loved us passionately.

Most winners are just ex-losers who got passionate. The worst bankruptcy in the world is the person who has lost his enthusiasm, his passion. When you add passion to a belief, it becomes a conviction. And there is a big difference between a belief and a conviction. Driven by passionate conviction, you can do anything you want with your life — except give up on the thing you care about. My friend, Mike Murdock, said, "What generates passion and zeal in you is a clue to revealing your destiny. What you love is a clue to something you contain."

Fulfilling God's plan for your life is a passion or it is nothing. "*Serve the Lord thy God with all thy heart and with*

all thy soul" (Deut. 10:12). "Without passion man is a mere latent force and a possibility, like the flint which awaits the shock of the iron before it can give forth its spark" (Henri Frederic Ameil). Pessimism never won any battles. "There are many things that will catch my eye, but there are only a very few that catch my heart...it is those I consider to pursue," said Tim Redmond.

NUGGET #9

Don't Ask Time Where It's Gone; Tell It Where To Go

All great achievers, all successful people, are those who have been able to gain control over their time. It has been said that all human beings have been created equal in one respect: each person has been given 24 hours each day.

We need to choose to give our best time to our most challenging situation. It's not how much we do that matters; it's how much we get done. We should choose to watch our time, not our watch. One of the best timesavers is the ability to say no. Not saying no when you should is one of the biggest wastes of time you will ever experience.

Don't spend a dollar's worth of time for ten cents' worth of results.

Make sure to take care of the vulnerable times in your days. These vulnerable times are the first thing in the morning and the last thing at night. I have heard a minister say that what a person is like at midnight when he is all alone reveals that person's true self.

Never allow yourself to say, "I could be doing big things if I weren't so busy doing small things!" Take control of your time. **The greater control you exercise over your time, the greater freedom you will experience in your life.** The psalmist prayed, *So teach us to number our days, that we may apply our hearts unto wisdom* (Ps. 90:12). The Bible teaches us that the devil comes to steal, and to kill, and to destroy (John 10:10), and this verse applies to time as well as to people. The enemy desires to provide God's children with ideas of how to kill, steal, and destroy valuable time.

People area always saying, "I'd give anything to be able to. . ." There is a basic leadership principle that says, "6 x 1 = 6." If you want to write a book, learn to play a musical instrument, become a better tennis player, or do anything else important, then you should devote one hour a day; six days a week, to the project. Sooner than you think, what you desire will become reality. There are not many things that a person cannot accomplish in 312 hours a year! Just a commitment of one hour a day, six days a week, is all it takes.

We all have the same amount of time each day. The difference between people is determined by what they do with the amount of time at their disposal. Don't be like the airline pilot flying over the Pacific Ocean who reported to his passengers, "We're lost, but we're making great time!" Remember that the future arrives an hour at a time. **Gain control of your time, and you will gain control of your life.**

NUGGET #10

Invest In Yourself

God, on a regular basis, sends across our paths divine opportunities for investment in ourselves. Be on the lookout for them. He does this first through His Word, which is the best investment we can put into ourselves. But He also sends many other "investment opportunities" to us. In my own life I've incorporated many of these. For example, my wife and I have a weekly "date night" which has been a great investment in our marriage. Also, every Saturday the kids and I "sneak out" on Mom to an early breakfast together. This time has been great for the kids and me, while allowing my wife a nice break.

Everything you say or do creates an investment somewhere. Whether that investment generates a dividend or a loss depends on you. **Always do your best, for what you plant now you will harvest later.**

One of the biggest mistakes you can make is to believe that you work for someone else. No matter how many bosses you may have, you really work for the Lord. You can't look to others as your source. That's why tapping into God's investment opportunities is so important. When an archer misses the mark, he looks for the fault within himself, not within the target. "To improve your aim — improve yourself" (Gilbert Arland).

When prosperity comes, do not use all of it. Give some back to others, and invest in yourself. **One half of knowing**

what you want is knowing what you must give up before you get it. Time invested in improving yourself precludes time wasted in disapproving others.

   "Study to show thyself approved unto God, a workman that needeth not to be ashamed" (2 Tim. 2:15). Investment doesn't cost, it pays. You cannot fulfill your destiny without applying the principle of investing in yourself.

NUGGET #11

Obey the Ninth Commandment

For those of us who are not Bible scholars, the essence of the Ninth Commandment can be summarized in one statement, "Thou shalt not lie." Each Christian should be a person of unquestionable integrity. For us, gray is never right; it must be either black or white.

Hope built on a lie is always the beginning of loss. Never attempt to build anything on a foundation of lies and half-truths. It will not stand.

It has been said that it should be easy to make an honest living because there is so little competition. Actually **only a person with honesty and integrity can be accurately motivated or directed.** Lying will always distort God's guidance in your life. It will cause you to take steps that are not right for you. It will produce greater loss than whatever savings you may gain by telling an untruth.

Lying becomes a very easy habit. The fact is that a person who allows himself to lie once will find it much easier to do so a second time. Lying is also a trap. No one has a good enough memory to be a successful liar. T.L. Osborn says, "Always tell the truth, and you never have to remember what you said."

In Proverbs 12:22 we read, *Lying lips are an abomination to the Lord: but they that deal truly are his delight.* Proverbs 19:9 declares, *A false witness shall not be unpunished, and he that*

speaketh lies shall perish. In Colossians 3:9,10 the Apostle Paul admonishes us:

Lie not one to another, seeing that ye have put off the old man with his deeds;

And have put on the new man, which is renewed in knowledge after the image of him that created him.

There are seven results of lying. If you lie:

1. You will attract liars into your life. (Prov. 17:4)

2. You will have a lack of understanding. (Ps. 119:104)

3. You will never enjoy permanent results. (Prov. 12:19; 21:28)

4. You will end up in bondage. (Gal. 2:4)

5. You will be punished. (Prov. 19:5)

6. You will become a fool. (Prov. 10:18)

7. Your lies will come back upon you. (Ps. 7:14-16)

Little white lies grow up to be big black lies. Decide and determine to be free from the bondage of breaking the Ninth Commandment.

NUGGET #12

"A Man With One Watch Knows What Time It Is; A Man With Two Is Never Quite Sure"

– Anonymous Quote

Have you ever noticed that some of the most miserable people in the world are those who can never make a decision? **When the human mind is in doubt, it is most easily swayed by the slightest of impulses.** This opens the door to many, many wrong decisions. Many times indecision allows things to go from bad to worse. Indecision is deadly. The truth is that the most dangerous place to be is in the middle of the road.

We believers should be the most decisive of all people. Christian leaders should have wills, not wishes. In James 1:8 the Bible says, *A double minded man is unstable in all his ways.* An indecisive person allows instability to creep into every area of his life. If we don't decide what is important in our own lives, we will probably end up doing only the things that are important to others. **The greater the degree of wishful thinking, the greater the degree of mediocrity.** Being decisive, being focused, committing ourselves to the fulfillment of a dream, greatly increases our probability of success. It also closes the door to wrong options.

The challenge for all of us is to be dedicated dreamers, or perhaps I should say, decisive dreamers. Harry Truman once said, "Some questions cannot be answered, but they can be decided." Most of the time, you and I may not have all the facts available about any given situation, but we will usually have all the facts we need to make a decision. The Bible says to let the peace of God rule in our hearts. (Col. 3:15.) *The Amplified Bible* version tells us to let the peace which comes from Christ act as an umpire in our hearts.

Be decisive. Go with the peace of God and do not be afraid to make a decision. The fact is that decisive people typically prevail and rise to the top because most people are indecisive.

If you are neutral on spiritual matters, you will likely find yourself operating against heaven. Thank God we serve a decisive Lord. He has given us His peace and His Word so we can make wise decisions. We should not be the kind of people who claim that God has told us one thing this week and the very opposite next week. God does not change His degrees that quickly. Nor does He ever direct anyone to act contrary to the good sense and sound judgment shown in His Word.

God desires that we be decisive in our lives. As His children we should be like our heavenly Father, with Whom there is *"no variableness, neither shadow of turning."* (James 1:17.) We should be people of great wills. **If the devil controls our will, he controls our destiny. But if God controls our will, then He controls our destiny.**

The choice is ours. Let's be decisive. Let's make the right decision!

NUGGET #13

Good Intentions Aren't
Good Enough

You can't test your destiny cautiously. "Don't play for safety — it's the most dangerous thing in the world," said Hugh Walpole. The key is this: to forfeit the safety of what we are for what we could become. Unless you do something beyond what you have already done, you will never grow.

A definition of "mediocrity": best of the worst and worst of the best. **"Potential" means you haven't done your best yet.** Good intentions are like checks that men try to draw from a bank where they have no account. Every mediocre person has good intentions.

It's been said that the biggest enemy of great is good. Don't accept good enough as good enough. Tolerating mediocrity in others makes me more mediocre. **Only an average person is always at his best.**

A man can't make a place for himself in the sun if he keeps taking refuge under the family tree. Go! Launch out! "People who never do any more than they get paid for never get paid for any more than they do," said Elbert Hubbard. Do more! An over-cautious person burns bridges of opportunity before he gets to them. Most of the people who sit around and wait for the harvest haven't planted anything. The average man doesn't want much and usually gets even less.

One action is more valuable than a thousand good intentions. "Security is mostly a superstition. It does not exist in nature, nor do the children of men as a whole experience it. Avoiding danger is no safer in the long run than outright exposure. Life is either a daring adventure, or nothing" (Helen Keller).

NUGGET #14

Don't Consume Your Tomorrows Feeding On Your Yesterdays

Decide today to get rid of any "loser's limps" which you may still be carrying from some past experience. As followers of Jesus Christ, you and I need to break the power of the past to dominate our present and determine our future.

In Luke 9:62, Jesus said, ...*No man, having put his hand to the plough, and looking back, is fit for the kingdom of God.* If we are not careful, we will allow the past to exercise a great hold on us. **The more we look backward, the less able we are to see forward.** The past makes no difference concerning what God can do for us today.

That is the beauty of the Christian life. Even when we have failed, we are able to ask for forgiveness and be totally cleansed of and released from our past actions. Whatever hold the past may have on us can be broken. It is never God who holds us back. It is always our own choosing to allow the past to keep us from living to the fullest in the present and future. Failure is waiting around the corner for those who are living off of yesterday's successes and failures. **We should choose to be forward-focused, not past-possessed.** We should learn to profit from the past, but to invest in the future.

In Philippians 3:13,14, the Apostle Paul writes:

Brethren, I count not myself to have apprehended: but this one thing I do, forgetting those things which are behind, and reaching forth unto those things which are before,

I press toward the mark for the prize of the high calling of God in Christ Jesus.

The key here is "forgetting those things which are behind" in order to reach for "the high calling of God in Christ Jesus." To fulfill our calling in Christ, we must first forget that which lies behind. Probably the most common stronghold in a person's life is his past mistakes and failures. Today is the day to begin to shake off the shackles of the past and move forward.

The past is past. It has no life.

NUGGET #15

Questions

"Who said it?" is an important question to ask of everything we believe.

Do you make promises or commitments?

Do you make friends before you need them?

Does God seem far away? If so, guess who moved?

Who's creating your world?

Do you have a strong will or a strong won't?

The last time you failed, did you stop trying because you failed — or did you fail because you stopped trying?

What is it like to be my friend?

What is it like to work with me?

Are you making a living or a life?

If the future generations were dependent on you for spiritual knowledge, how much would they receive?

Do you risk enough to exercise your faith in God?

Do you say "our Father" on Sunday and then act like an orphan the rest of the week?

Are you willing to preach what you practice?

Does failure discourage or bring determination?

Do you exist, or do you live?

Is God your hope or your excuse?

What dominates your day?

How many people have made you homesick to know God?

Is your mission on earth finished?

How many happy selfish people do you know?

How many people do you know who became successful at something they hate?

What force is more potent than love?

"Is any thing too hard for the Lord?" (Gen. 18:14).

If you were arrested for being kind, would there be enough evidence to convict you?

What is more miserable than being out of God's will?

NUGGET #16

The Best Time of Day Is Now

Procrastination is a killer.

When you choose to kill time, you begin to kill those gifts and callings which God has placed within your life. *The Living Bible* paraphrase of Ecclesiastes 11:4 reads: *If you wait for perfect conditions, you will never get anything done.*

The first step in overcoming procrastination is to eliminate all excuses and reasons for not taking decisive and immediate action.

Everybody is on the move. They are moving forwards, backwards, or on a treadmill. The mistake most people make is thinking that the main goal of life is to stay busy. Such thinking is a trap. What is important is not whether a person is busy, but whether he is progressing. It is a question of activity versus accomplishment.

A gentleman named John Henry Fabre conducted an experiment with processionary caterpillars. They are so named because of their peculiar habit of blindly following each other no matter how they are lined up or where they are going. This man took a group of these tiny creatures and did something interesting with them. He placed them in a circle. For 24 hours the caterpillars dutifully followed one another around and around. Then he did something else. He placed the caterpillars around a saucer full of pine needles (their favorite food). For six days the mindless creatures moved around and around the saucer, literally dying from starvation and exhaustion even though an abundance of choice food was located less than two inches away.

You see, they had confused activity with accomplishment.

We Christians need to be known as those who accomplish great things for God — not those who simply talk about it. Procrastinators are good at talking versus doing. It is true what Mark Twain said: "Noise produces nothing. Often a hen who has merely laid an egg cackles as though she has laid an asteroid."

We need to be like the apostles. They were never known much for their policies or procedures, their theories or excuses. Instead, they were known for their acts. Many people say that they are waiting for God; but in most cases God is waiting for them. We need to say with the psalmist, "Lord, my times are in Your hands." (Ps. 31:15.) The price of growth is always less than the cost of stagnation. As Edmund Burke said, "The only thing necessary for the triumph of evil is for good men to do nothing."

Occasionally you may see someone who doesn't do anything, and yet seems to be successful in life. Don't be deceived. The old saying is true: "Even a broken clock is right twice a day." As Christians we are called to make progress — not excuses.

Procrastination is a primary tool of the devil to hold us back and to make us miss God's timing in our lives. *The desire of the slothful killeth him; for his hands refuse to labour* (Prov. 21:25). **The fact is, the longer we take to act on God's direction, the more unclear it becomes.**

NUGGET #17

Fear And Worry Are Interest Paid in Advance On Something You May Never Own

Fear is a poor chisel to carve out tomorrow. Worry is simply the triumph of fear over faith.

There's a story that is told about a woman who was standing on a street corner crying profusely. A man came up to her and asked why she was weeping. The lady shook her head and replied: "I was just thinking that maybe someday I would get married. We would later have a beautiful baby girl. Then one day this child and I would go for a walk along this street, come to this corner, and my darling daughter would run into the street, get hit by a car, and die."

Now that sounds like a pretty ridiculous situation — for a grown woman to be weeping her eyes out because of something that would probably never happen. Yet isn't this the way we respond when we worry? We take a situation or event which might never exist and build it up all out of proportion in our mind.

There is an old Swedish proverb that says, "Worry gives a small thing a big shadow." **Worry is simply the misuse of God's creative imagination which He has placed within each of us.** When fear rises in our mind, we should learn to expect the opposite in our life.

The word *worry* itself is derived from an Anglo-Saxon term meaning "to strangle," or "to choke off." There is no question that worry and fear in the mind does choke off the creative flow from above. Things are seldom as they seem. "Skim milk masquerades as cream," said W.S. Gilbert. As we dwell on and worry about matters beyond our control, a negative effect begins to set in. Too much analysis always leads to paralysis. **Worry is a route which leads from somewhere to nowhere. Don't let it direct your life.**

In Psalm 55:22 the Bible says, *Cast thy burden upon the Lord, and he shall sustain thee: he shall never suffer the righteous to be moved.* Never respond out of fear, and never fear to respond. Action attacks fear; inaction builds fear.

Don't worry and don't fear. Instead, take your fear and worry to the Lord, *Casting all your care upon him; for he careth for you* (1 Pet. 5:7).

NUGGET #18

A Goal Is A Dream
With A Deadline

In Habakkuk 2:2 the Lord tells the prophet, ...*Write the vision, and make it plain upon tables, that he may run that readeth it.* The key to successful goal-setting is revealed in this scripture.

First, the vision must be written down. When you keep a vision in your mind, it is not really a goal; it is really nothing more than a dream. There is power in putting that dream down on paper. When you commit something to writing, commitment to achievement naturally follows. You can't start a fire with paper alone, but writing something down on paper can start a fire inside of you.

God Himself followed His Word here, by taking His vision for us and having it put down on paper in the form of the Bible. He did not just rely on the Holy Spirit to guide and direct us; He put His goals down in writing. We are told to make the word of the Lord plain upon "tables" (tablets) so that it is clear and specific as to what the vision is "...so that he may run that readeth it."

The key word is "run." God desires that we run with the vision and goal in our life. As long as we are running with the vision, we won't turn around. When you walk with a vision, it's easy to change directions and go the wrong way. **You can't stroll to a goal.**

In Proverbs 24:3,4 (TLB), we read: *Any enterprise is built by wise planning, becomes strong through common sense, and profits wonderfully by keeping abreast of the facts.* Simply stated, effective goal-setting and planning provides an opportunity to bring the future to the present and deal with it today. You will find that achievement is easy when your outer goals become an inner commitment.

Even though we have the Holy Spirit, we still need to prepare; we are just better equipped to do so. God's first choice for us in any situation cannot be disorder and waste of funds or resources. That's why proper planning is so important. Plan to the potential. Believe for God's biggest dream. When you plan, look to the future, not the past. You can't drive forward by looking out the rear window.

Always involve yourself with something that's bigger than you are, because that's where God is. Every great success was, at the beginning, impossible. We all have opportunity for success in our lives. It takes just as much energy and effort for a bad life as it does for a good life; yet most people live meaningless lives simply because they never decided to write their vision down and then follow through on it. Know this, if you can't see the mark, you can't press towards it.

Ponder the path of thy feet, and let all thy ways be established (Prov. 4:26). You will find that what you learn on the path to your goals is actually more valuable than achieving the goal itself. Columbus discovered America while searching for a route to India. Be on the lookout for the "Americas" in your path. Put God's vision for your life on paper, and begin to run with His plan.

NUGGET #19

The Best Helping Hand You Will Ever Find Is At the End of Your Own Arm

One of the biggest lies of the world is that we are not responsible for our own actions. We are told that it's our mother's fault, our employer's fault, our neighbor's fault, the government's fault, society's fault. But in Romans 14:12, the Bible clearly indicates who is responsible and accountable for our deeds: *So then every one of us shall give account of himself to God.*

We may want or even attempt to shift the blame to others, but there is no escaping the truth: when we point the finger at someone else, there are three fingers pointing back at ourselves.

Throughout my career as a consultant, I have met with many businessmen who were looking everywhere for answers. It was amazing to me how many were anxiously searching for help from other people while they had — between them and God — everything they needed to succeed. They were easily willing to give up control of their vision to others in exchange for money or even companionship. Their mistake was in looking to others instead of God.

This kind of false security invariably leads to imbalanced relationships which eventually result in destruction of the person and his dream.

Now I believe that God sends people across our path to bless us and help us. But we should be directed by God and be very cautious when entering into any partnership relationship. We must be sure that the reason for the relationship is right; that it is not an attempt to compromise or look for a shortcut.

For every successful partnership, there are hundreds that were disasters. Exercise great caution when affiliating with someone else. In Exodus, God gave Moses some good advice that is applicable to us as Christians today. He said, *"Be careful not to make a treaty with those who live in the land where you are going, or they will be a snare among you"* (Ex. 34:12 NIV).

I believe that most of the things God wants to teach us, He wants us to learn for ourselves. Mark Twain said, "A man who carries a cat by the tail learns something he can learn no other way."

Decide for yourself. Learn for yourself. Answer for yourself.

NUGGET #20

Today I Will. . .

Rise early because no day is long enough for a day's work.

Compliment three people.

Make myself valuable to somebody.

Not lose an hour in the morning and spend all day looking for it.

Tackle a problem bigger than me.

Make a small improvement in some area.

Change my thinking from TGIF to TGIT—Thank God It's Today!

Do at least three things that will take me out of my comfort zone.

Die to myself.

Give thanks for my daily bread.

Find something different to do.

Leave someone a little better than I found them.

Give my best time to communion with God.

Live by the Golden Rule so I won't have to apologize for my actions tomorrow.

Know that the place to be happy is here, the time to be happy is now.

Take small steps to conquer a bad habit.

Judge this day, not by the harvest, but by the seeds I plant.

NUGGET #21

Our Words Are Seeds Planted Into Other People's Lives

What we say is important. The Bible states that out of the abundance of the heart the mouth speaks. (Matt. 12:34.) We need to change our vocabulary. We need to speak words of life and light. Our talk should always rise to the level of the Word of God.

We Christians should be known as people who speak positively, those who speak the Word of God into situations, those who speak forth words of life.

We should not be like the man who joined a monastery in which the monks were allowed to speak only two words every seven years. After the first seven years had passed, the new initiate met with the abbot who asked him, "Well, what are your two words?"

"Food's bad," replied the man, who then went back to spend another seven-year period before once again meeting with his ecclesiastical superior.

"What are your two words now?" asked the clergyman.

"Bed's hard," responded the man.

Seven years later — twenty-one years after his initial entry into the monastery — the man met with the abbot for the third and final time.

"And what are your two words this time?" he was asked.

"I quit."

"Well, I'm not surprised," answered the disgusted cleric, "all you've done since you got here is complain!"

Don't be like that man; don't be known as a person whose only words are negative.

If you are a member of the "murmuring grapevine," you need to resign. In John 6:43 our Lord instructed His disciples, *...Murmur not among yourselves.* In Philippians 2:14,15 the Apostle Paul exhorted the believers of his day:

Do all things without murmurings and disputings:

That ye may be blameless and harmless, the sons of God, without rebuke, in the midst of a crooked and perverse nation, among whom ye shine as lights in the world.

Contrary to what you may have heard, talk is not cheap. Talk is very expensive. We should know that our words are powerful. What we say affects what we get from others, and what others get from us. When we speak the wrong word, it lessens our ability to see and hear the will of God.

NUGGET #22

The Most Natural Thing To Do When You Get Knocked Down Is To Get Up

---

How we respond to failure and mistakes is one of the most important decisions we make every day. Failure doesn't mean that nothing has been accomplished. There is always the opportunity to learn something. What is in you will always be bigger than whatever is around you.

We all experience failure and make mistakes. In fact, successful people always have more failure in their lives than average people do. You will find that throughout history all great people, at some point in their lives, have failed. **Only those who do not expect anything are never disappointed. Only those who never try, never fail.** Anyone who is currently achieving anything in life is simultaneously risking failure. It is always better to fail in doing something than to excel in doing nothing. A flawed diamond is more valuable than a perfect brick. People who have no failures also have few victories.

Everybody gets knocked down, it's how fast he gets up that counts. There is a positive correlation between spiritual maturity and how quickly a person responds to his failures and mistakes. The greater the degree of spiritual maturity, the greater the ability to get back up and go on. The less the spiritual maturity, the longer the individual will continue to hang on to past failures. Every person knows someone who, to this day, is still held back by mistakes he made years ago. God never sees any of us as failures; He only sees us as learners.

We have only failed when we do not learn from the experience. The decision is up to us. We can choose to turn a failure into a hitching post, or a guidepost.

Here is the key to being free from the stranglehold of past failures and mistakes: learn the lesson and forget the details. Gain from the experience, but do not roll over and over in your mind the minute details of it. Build on the experience, and get on with your life.

Remember: **the call is higher than the fall.**

NUGGET #23

Those Who Don't Take Chances Don't Make Advances

All great discoveries have been made by people whose faith ran ahead of their minds. Significant achievements have not been obtained by taking small risks on unimportant issues. Don't ever waste time planning, analyzing, and risking on small ideas. It is always wise to spend more time on decisions that are irreversible and less time on those that are reversible.

Learn to stretch, to reach out where God is. Aim high and take risks. The world's approach is to look to next year based on last year. We Christians need to reach to the potential, not reckon to the past. Those who make great strides are those who take chances and plan toward the challenges of life.

Don't become so caught up in small matters that you can't take advantage of important opportunities. Most people spend their entire lives letting down buckets into empty wells. They continue to waste away their days trying to draw them up again.

Choose today to dream big, to strive to reach the full potential of your calling. Choose to major on the important issues of life, not on the unimportant. H. Stern said, "If you're hunting rabbits in tiger country, you must keep your eye peeled for tigers, but when you are hunting tigers you can ignore the rabbits." There are plenty of tigers to go around.

Don't be distracted by or seek after the rabbits of life. Set your sights on "big game."

Security and opportunity are total strangers. If an undertaking doesn't include faith, it's not worthy of being called God's direction. I don't believe that God would call any of us to do anything that would not include an element of faith in Him.

There is a famous old saying that goes, "Even a turtle doesn't get ahead unless he sticks his neck out." **Dream big, because you serve a big God.**

NUGGET #24

"Remember That The Faith To Move Mountains Always Carries A Pick"
– Anonymous Quote

Rising above mediocrity never just happens, it is always a result of faith combined with works.

Faith without works is like gold within the earth. It is of no value until it is worked and mined out. **A person who has faith without actions is like a bird with wings but no feet.** In James 2:17 the Bible says, *Even so faith, if it hath not works, is dead, being alone.*

Biblical principles times nothing equals nothing.

We believers need to be people who put our faith into action. One individual with faith and action constitutes a majority. Don't wait for your ship to come in — swim out to it. Thomas Edison said it best when he noted, "Opportunity is missed by most people because it is dressed in overalls and looks like work." True faith has hands and feet; it takes action. It's not enough to "know that you know." It's more important to show that you know.

The word *work* appears in the Bible 564 times. So work is not a vague scriptural concept. When faith and works operate together, the result is a masterpiece. We should choose to keep our faith working all the time and not quit. George Bernard Shaw said, "When I was young I observed that nine out of every ten things I did were failures. So I did ten times more work."

The founder of Holiday Inns, Kemin Wilson, when asked how he became successful, replied, "I really don't know why I'm here. I never got a degree, and I've only worked half days my entire life. I guess my advice is to do the same, work half days every day. And it doesn't matter which half. The first twelve hours or the second twelve hours." Tap into the power that is produced when faith is mixed with action, and then watch God move in your situation.

NUGGET #25

Smile. It Adds To Your Face Value

Christians should be the happiest, most enthusiastic, people on earth. In fact, the word enthusiasm comes from a Greek word, *entheous* which means "God within" or "full of God."

Smiling — being happy and enthusiastic — is always a choice and not a result. It is a decision that must be consciously made. Enthusiasm and joy and happiness will improve your personality and people's opinion of you. It will help you keep a proper perspective on life. Helen Keller said, "Keep your face to the sunshine and you cannot see the shadow."

The bigger the challenge you are facing, the more enthusiasm you need. Philippians 2:5 (NIV) says, *Your attitude should be the same as that of Christ Jesus.* I believe Jesus was a man Who had a smile on His face, a spring in His step, and joy on His countenance.

Our attitude always tells others what we expect in return.

A smile is a powerful weapon. It can even break the ice. You'll find that being happy and enthusiastic is like a head cold — it's very, very contagious. A laugh a day will keep negative people away. You will also find that as enthusiasm increases, stress and fear in your life willdecrease. The Bible says that the joy of the Lord is our strength. (Neh. 8:10.)

Many people say, "Well, no wonder that person is happy, confident, and positive; if I had his job and assets, I would be too." Such thinking falsely assumes that successful people are positive because they have a good income and lots of possessions. But the reverse is true. Such people probably have a good income and lots of possessions as a result of being positive, confident, and happy.

Enthusiasm always motivates to action. No significant accomplishment has ever been made without enthusiasm. In John 15:10,11 (NIV) we have a promise from the Lord, *"If you obey my commands, you will remain in my love, just as I have obeyed my Father's commands and remain in his love. I have told you this so that my joy may be in you and that your joy may be complete."*

The joy and love of the Lord are yours — so smile!

NUGGET #26

We Can Grow by our Questions, As Well As By Our Answers

Here are some important questions we should ask ourselves:

1. What one decision would I make if I knew that it would not fail?

2. What one thing should I eliminate from my life because it holds me back from reaching my full potential?

3. Am I on the path of something absolutely marvelous, or something absolutely mediocre?

4. If everyone in the United States of America were on my level of spirituality, would there be a revival in the land?

5. Does the devil know who I am?

6. Am I running from something, or to something?

7. What can I do to make better use of my time?

8. Would I recognize Jesus if I met Him on the street?

9. Who do I need to forgive?

10. What is my favorite scripture for myself, my family, my career?

11. What impossible thing am I believing and planning for?

12. What is my most prevailing thought?

13. What good thing have I previously committed myself to do that I have quit doing?

14. Of the people I respect most, what is it about them that earns my respect?

15. What would a truly creative person do in my situation?

16. What outside influences are causing me to be better or worse?

17. Can I lead anyone else to Christ?

18. In what areas do I need improvement in terms of personal development?

19. What gifts, talents, or strengths do I have?

20. What is one thing that I can do for someone else who has no opportunity to repay me?

NUGGET #27

The Person With Imagination Is Never Alone and Never Finished

You were created for creativity. Your eyes look for opportunity, your ears listen for direction, your mind requires a challenge and your heart longs for God's way.

Make a daily demand on your creativity. **Everything great started as somebody's daydream.** All people of action are first dreamers. The wonder of imagination is this: It has the power to light its own fire. Ability is a flame, creativity is a fire. Originality sees things with fresh vision. Unlike an airplane, your imagination can take off day or night in any kind of circumstances.

First Corinthians 2:16 says, "We have the mind of Christ."

A genius is someone who shoots at a target no one else sees and hits it. "We are told never to cross a bridge till we come to it, but this world is owned by men who have 'crossed bridges' in their imagination far ahead of the crowd" (Speakers Library). We should observe the future and act before it occurs. Many times we act, or fail to act, not because of will but because of imagination. A person's dreams are an indicator of his potential greatness. **A God-given idea always comes to an individual with the force of a revelation.**

Grandmother saw Billy running around the house slapping himself and asked him why. "Well," said Billy, "I just got so tired of walking that I thought I'd ride my horse for a while."

One day Michelangelo saw a block of marble which the owner said was of no value. "It is valuable to me," said Michelangelo. "There is an angel imprisoned in it, and I must set it free."

Other people may be smarter, better educated or more experienced than you, but no single person has a corner on dreams, desire or ambition. The creation of a thousand forests of opportunity spring from a tiny acorn of an idea. "No man that does not see visions will ever realize any high hope or undertake any high enterprise," said Woodrow Wilson. The Bible says, "Where there is no vision, the people perish" (Prov. 29:18). A dream is one of the most exciting things there is. You are more than an empty bottle to be filled. **You are a candle to be lit.** Your heart has eyes which the brain knows nothing of.

NUGGET #28

"If You Continue To Do What's Right, What's Wrong and Who's Wrong Will Eventually Leave Your Life" – David Blunt

A businessman had personalized letterhead that read: "Right is right even if everyone is against it, and wrong is wrong even if everyone is for it." James 1:12 (TLB) says, "Happy is the man who doesn't give in and do wrong when he is tempted, for afterwards he will get as his reward the crown of life that God has promised those who love him."

Spend less time worrying about who's right and take charge of deciding what's right in your life. Don't let someone else choose it for you. Your failures may be planned by hell, but your victory is planned by heaven. "And remember, when someone wants to do wrong it is never God who is tempting him, for God never wants to do wrong and never tempts anyone else to do it" (James 1:13, TLB).

You cannot do the right thing too soon, for you never know when it will be too late. You can always find the time to do what you really want to do. Successful people understand that no one makes it to the top in a single bound. What sets them apart is their willingness to keep putting the right step in front of the other, no matter how rough the terrain. We are what we repeatedly do.

Consider the words of John Wesley:

Do all the good you can,
In all the ways you can,
In all the places you can,
At all times you can,
To all the people you can,
As long as ever you can.

You draw nothing out of the bank of life except what you deposit in it. **The height of a man's potential is in proportion to his surrender to what is right.** People who live right never get left. Any act of disobedience lengthens the distance between you and your dream. Likewise, no problem can stand the assault of sustained prayer and right action.

NUGGET #29

An Alibi Is Just A Lie

Quitting, giving up, failing, judging — all these begin with an excuse. Never allow an obstacle in your life to become an alibi — which is simply egotism turned the wrong side out.

You, therefore, have no excuse, you who pass judgment on someone else, for at whatever point you judge the other, you are condemning yourself, because you who pass judgment do the same things (Rom. 2:1 NIV). We Christians should be people who make progress, not excuses. When we alibi, we always point the blame somewhere else. This causes further judgment to come our way.

There have always been people who have tried to make excuses to the Lord. Some knew that their alibis were not true. And then there were those who made excuses and actually believed them; these ended up in much different circumstances.

In Luke 14:18-20 (NIV) Jesus told a parable of the great end-time banquet and the men who were invited to the Lord's table:

"But they all alike began to make excuses. The first said, 'I have just bought a field, and I must go to see it. Please excuse me.'"

"Another said, 'I have just bought five yoke of oxen, and I'm on my way to try them out. Please excuse me.'"

"Still another said, 'I just got married, so I can't come.'"

77

These men alibied and missed out on salvation. All of them made the mistake of believing their alibis rather than God.

Two other men in the Bible, Moses and Gideon, also made excuses to the Lord. The difference is that, although they alibied, they recognized that their excuses were not the truth. Moses tried to alibi to God. In Exodus 4:10-12 (NIV), he said:

...“O Lord, I have never been eloquent, neither in the past nor since you have spoken to your servant. I am slow of speech and tongue.”

The Lord said to him, “Who gave man his mouth? Who makes him deaf or dumb? Who gives him sight or makes him blind? Is it not I, the Lord? Now go; I will help you speak and will teach you what to say.”

Gideon, in Judges 6:15 (NIV), argued:

“But Lord,...how can I save Israel? My clan is the weakest in Manasseh, and I am the least in my family.”

The Lord answered, “I will be with you, and you will strike down the Midianites as if they were but one man.”

When you are confronted with an alibi, do as Moses and Gideon: choose to believe God, and not the excuse. In John 15:22 (NIV), Jesus said, “If I had not come and spoken to them, they would not be guilty of sin. Now, however, they have no excuse for their sin.”

Recognize an alibi for what it is — a sin against God.

NUGGET #30

Don't Quit After A Victory

There are two times when a person stops: after a defeat and after a victory. Eliminating this kind of procrastination increases momentum.

Robert Schuller has a good saying: "Don't cash in, cast into deeper water." Don't stop after a success, keep the forward momentum going.

One of the great prizes of victory is the opportunity to do more. The trouble is, we've innoculated ourselves with small doses of success which keep us from catching the real thing.

As I was writing this section on momentum, I couldn't get out of my mind a picture of a large boulder at the top of a hill. This boulder represents our lives. If we rock the boulder back and forth and get it moving, its momentum will make it almost unstoppable. The same is true of us.

The Bible promises us God's divine momentum in our lives. In Philippians 1:6 the Apostle Paul writes, *Being confident of this very thing, that he which hath begun a good work in you will perform it until the day of Jesus Christ.* God's momentum always results in growth.

There are five ways to have divine momentum in your life:

1. Be fruitful. (2 Cor. 9:10.)

2. Speak the truth. (Eph. 4:15.)

3. Be spiritually mature. (Heb. 6:1.)

4. Crave the Word of God. (1 Pet. 2:2.)

5. Grow in the grace and knowledge of Jesus. (2 Pet. 3:18.)

God's definition of spiritual momentum is found in 2 Peter 1:5 (NIV):

For this very reason, make every effort to add to your faith goodness; and to goodness, knowledge; and to knowledge, self-control; and to self-control, perseverance; and to perseverance, godliness; and to godliness, brotherly kindness; and to brotherly kindness, love. For if you possess these qualities in increasing measure, they will keep you from being ineffective and unproductive in your knowledge of our Lord Jesus Christ.

Let go of whatever makes you stop.

NUGGET #31

Versus

Every day we make decisions. Daily we are confronted with options. **We must choose one or the other.** We cannot have both. These options include:

Being bitter versus being better.

Indifference versus decisiveness.

Lukewarmness versus enthusiasm.

"If we can" versus "how we can."

"Give up" versus "get up."

Security versus risk.

Coping with evil versus overcoming evil.

Blending in versus standing out.

How much we do versus how much we get done.

Coexisting with darkness versus opposing darkness.

Destruction versus development.

Resisting versus receiving.

Complaining versus obtaining.

Trying versus committing.

Peace versus strife.

Choice versus chance.

Determination versus discouragement.

Growing versus dying.

Demanding more of ourselves versus excusing ourselves.

Doing for others versus doing for self.

Progress versus regression.

Steering versus drifting.

Priorities versus aimlessness.

Accountability versus irresponsibility.

Action versus activity.

Solutions versus problems.

More of God versus more of everything else.

Being in "Who's Who" versus asking "Why me?"

NUGGET #32

Unforgiveness Has No Foresight

The one guaranteed formula for choking off originality is unforgiveness. "Never cut what can be untied" (Joseph Joubert). **When you have been wronged, a poor memory is your best response.** Never carry a grudge. While you're straining under its weight, the other guy's out producing.

Forgive your enemies — nothing annoys them more. There is no revenge so sweet as forgiveness. The only people you should try to get even with are those who have helped you.

"Forgiveness ought to be like a canceled note — torn in two, and burned up, so that it never can be shown against one" (Henry Ward Beecher). Never is God operating in your life so strong as when you forego revenge and dare to forgive an injury. "He who cannot forgive, destroys the bridge over which he may one day need to pass," said Larry Bielat. Hate, bitterness and revenge are luxuries you cannot afford.

People need loving most when they deserve it least. **Forgiveness heals; unforgiveness wounds.** Matthew 5:25 (TLB) says, "Come to terms quickly with your enemy before it is too late."

You can't get ahead when you're trying to get even. **Being offended is Satan's snare to get you out of the will of God.** When we think about our offense, trouble grows; when we think about God, trouble goes.

When you don't forgive, you are ignoring its impact on your destiny. "Hate is a prolonged form of suicide" (Douglas V. Steere). How much more grievous are the consequences of unforgiveness than the causes of it! "Life is an adventure in forgiveness," says author Norman Cousins. "Every person should have a special cemetery lot in which to bury the faults of friends and loved ones. To forgive is to set a prisoner free and discover the prisoner was you" (Unknown).

It's true that the one who forgives ends the quarrel. Patting a fellow on the back is the best way to get a chip off his shoulder. Forgive your enemies — you can't get back at them any other way! Forgiveness saves the expense of anger, the high cost of hatred and the waste of energy. **There are two marks of a Christian: giving and forgiving.**

If you want to be miserable, hate somebody. Unforgiveness does a great deal more damage to the vessel in which it is stored than the object on which it is poured.

NUGGET #33

Keep Your Feet On The Rock When You Reach The End of Your Rope

Don't quit. There is a big difference between quitting and changing. I believe that **when God sees someone who doesn't quit, He looks down and says, "There is someone I can use."**

In Galatians 6:9 (NIV) we are told, *Let us not become weary in doing good, for at the proper time we will reap a harvest if we do not give up.* Look at this verse carefully. It urges us not to become weary, assuring us that we will — not might — reap a harvest if we do not give up.

God doesn't quit. It is impossible for Him to do so. In Philippians 1:6 (NIV) the Apostle Paul writes about *being confident of this, that he who began a good work in you will carry it on to completion until the day of Christ Jesus.* There are several important points in this verse. The most crucial is the fact that God does not quit. Therefore, we can have great confidence that He will complete the good work He has begun in us. He will see us through every step of the way until we have reached our ultimate destination.

One of the best scriptural examples of a person who did not quit is Joseph. He had many reasons to justify giving up. First, when he was trapped in the pit into which his brothers had thrown him because of their jealousy, I am sure he said to himself, "This is not the way I dreamed my life would work out." Later on, he had a marvelous opportunity to become discouraged and quit when he was unjustly accused and thrown into prison for a crime he did not commit. Again he could have said to himself, "This is not right; I'm not supposed to be here."

But eventually the dream which God had given Joseph became reality. He was elevated from prisoner to prime minister in one day. Although Joseph did not know or understand the steps through which the Lord would lead him, he remained true to his God. Despite the trials and obstacles he faced, he did not quit.

There is no greater reward than that which comes as a result of holding fast to the Word and will of God. Only you can decide not to lose. Most people quit right on the verge of success. Often it is right at their fingertips. There is only one degree of difference between hot water and steam.

In Luke 18 (NIV) Jesus told the parable of the persistent widow. The Bible reveals His purpose in relating this story: *Then Jesus told his disciples a parable to show them they should always pray and not give up* (v. 1). The psalmist tells us, *Commit thy way unto the Lord; trust also in him; and he shall bring it to pass* (Ps. 37:5).

The only way we can lose is to quit. That is the only decision we can make that can keep us from reaching God's goals in our lives.

NUGGET #34

Be Like Babies. . . They Like Changes

The late astronaut James Irwin said, "You might think going to the moon was the most scientific project ever but they literally 'threw us' in the direction of the moon. We had to adjust our course every ten minutes and landed only inside fifty feet of the five hundred mile radius of our target." Life is full of changes.

"When you can't change the direction of the wind — adjust your sails" (Max DePree). We cannot become what we need to be by remaining what we are. **People hate change, yet it is the only thing that brings growth.** There is nothing so permanent as change.

Everyone wants to change the world, but no one thinks of changing themselves. "Poverty and shame shall be to him that refuseth instruction: but he that regardeth reproof shall be honoured" (Prov. 13:18). Unacceptance of the present creates a future. "Happy is the man whom God correcteth" (Job 5:17). "Better to be pruned to grow than cut up to burn," said John Trapp. A bad habit never goes away by itself. "It's always an undo-it-yourself project" (Abigail Van Buren).

Proverbs 13:19 (TLB) says, "It is pleasant to see plans develop. That is why fools refuse to give them up even when they are wrong." Wise people sometimes change their minds

— fools never do. **Be open to God's change in your plans. It is a sign of strength to make changes when necessary.**

The longer a man is in error, the surer he is he's right. Defending your faults and errors only proves that you have no intention of quitting them. An obstinate man does not hold opinions — they hold him. He who stops changing ceases growing.

Where we cannot invent we can at least improve. A "sensational new idea" is sometimes just an old idea with its sleeves rolled up. If you itch for ideas, keep on scratching. Everybody is in favor of progress. It's the change they don't like. Constant change is here to stay. Most people are willing to change, not because they see the light, but because they feel the heat.

Great ideas still need change, adaptation and modification in order to prosper and succeed. Henry Ford forgot to put a reverse gear in his first automobile. Few knew of his oversight. Few don't know of his success. **Success and growth are unlikely if you always do things the way you've always done them.**

NUGGET #35

Don't Build A Case Against Yourself

What does God think about your future? We find the answer in the book of Jeremiah (29:11, NIV): "I know the plans I have for you, declares the Lord, plans to prosper you and not to harm you, plans to give you hope and a future." All of what we are, good and bad, is what we have thought and believed. What you have become is due to the price you paid to get what you used to want.

All of the important battles we face will be waged within ourselves. Nothing great has ever been achieved except by those who dared believe that God was superior to any circumstance. First John 4:4 says, "Greater is he that is in you, than he who is in the world."

Don't put water in your own boat; the storm will put enough in on its own. **Don't dream up thousands of reasons why you can't do what you want to; find one reason why you can.** It is easier to do all the things you should do than spend the rest of your life wishing you had. The first key victory you must win is over yourself. "You can't consistently perform in a manner that is inconsistent with the way you see yourself," says Zig Ziglar.

Building a case against yourself is like a microscope — it magnifies trifling things but cannot receive great ones. To keep from building a case against yourself: multiply your prayer time, divide the truth from a lie, subtract negative influences and add God's Word. **We lie loudest when we lie to ourselves.** Both faith and fear may sail into your harbor, but allow only faith to drop anchor.

NUGGET #36

In The Race For Excellence There Is No Finish Line

Commit yourself to excellence from the start. No legacy is so rich as excellence. **The quality of your life will be in direct proportion to your commitment to excellence, regardless of what you choose to do.** "It's a funny thing about life; if you refuse to accept anything but the best, you very often get it," said Somerset Maugham. It takes less time to do something right than it does to explain why you did it wrong. "There is an infinite difference between a little wrong and just right, between fairly good and the best, between mediocrity and superiority," said Orison Swett Marcen.

Every day we should ask ourselves, "Why should my boss hire me instead of someone else?" or "Why should people do business with me instead of my competitors?" "Watch your actions; they become habits. Watch your habits; they become character. Watch your character; it becomes your destiny," said Frank Outlaw.

"Sin has many tools, but a lie is the handle that fits them all," said Oliver Wendell Holmes. Those who are given to white lies soon become color blind. **When you stretch the truth, watch out for the snap back.** A lie has no legs to support itself — it requires other lies. Beware of a half-truth; you may get hold of the wrong half. Each time you are honest, you propel yourself toward greater success. Each time you lie, even a little white lie, you push yourself toward failure.

Outside forces don't control your character. The measure of a person's real character is what he would do if he knew he would never be found out. Be more concerned with your character than with your reputation because your character is what you really are while your reputation is merely what others think you are. There is no right way to do the wrong thing.

"He that is good will infallibly become better, and he that is bad will as certainly become worse; for vice, virtue and time are three things that never stand still," said Charles Caleb Colton. Recently, I saw a plaque that said, "Excellence can be attained if you...care more than others think is wise, risk more than others think is safe, dream more than others think is practical, expect more than others think is possible." Excellence — it's contagious...be a leader...start an epidemic!

NUGGET #37

Turn The Bricks Others Throw At You Into Stepping Stones

All great ideas create conflict. In other words, your destiny creates challenges and criticism. Every great idea has three stages of response:

- "It is impossible — don't waste the time and the money."

- "It is possible but has a limited value."

- "I said it was a good idea all along."

A critic is like an armless man who teaches throwing. **While throwing mud, critics are simultaneously losing ground.** Foes and critics are never interested in solving the problem, and they never offer a better solution.

Our response to critics should be what the Bible says in 2 Corinthians 4:8,9: "We are perplexed, but not in despair; persecuted, but not forsaken; cast down, but not destroyed."

Criticism of Christians is the language of the devil. The Bible says the devil is the accuser of the brethren. Therefore we should consider that "He that is without sin among you, let him first cast a stone," (John 8:7). Attention men: Before you criticize another, look closely at your sister's brother!

It is the still small voice that we should follow, not the screeching blasts of doom. **Criticism is always a part of supernatural promotion.** If your head sticks up above the crowd, expect more criticism than bouquets. Satan always attacks those who can hurt him the most. God works from the inside out; the devil tries to work from the outside in.

Whoever criticizes to you will criticize about you. If someone belittles you, he is only trying to cut you down to his size. A statue has never been set up to a critic.

You can always tell a failure by the way he criticizes success. Those who can — do. Those who can't — criticize. Those who complain about the way the ball bounces are often the ones who dropped it. **If it were not for the doers, the critics would soon be out of business.** Envy provides the mud that failures throw at success. Small minds are the first to condemn great ideas.

If people talk negatively about you, live so that no one will believe them. Fear of criticism is the kiss of death in the courtship of achievement. **If you are afraid of criticism, you'll die doing nothing.** A successful man is one who can lay a firm foundation with the bricks that others throw at him.

NUGGET #38

Destiny Delayed Is The Devil's Delight

The most important moment in your life is right now. Don't let hesitation and procrastination keep you from your destiny. Procrastination is the symptom, fear is the problem. When you delay your duties, you delight the devil.

Be jealous of your time; it is your greatest treasure. **Ideas have a short shelf life — that's why we must act before the expiration date.** Procrastination is the ability to keep up with yesterday. "Even if you're on the right track — you'll get run over if you just sit there," says Arthur Godfrey. Putting off a simple thing makes it hard, and putting off a hard thing makes it impossible.

Obedience is God's method of provision for your life. "If ye be willing and obedient, ye shall eat the good of the land" (Is. 1:19). Obedience brings blessings. Discouragement always follows a decision to delay action.

Today is the day to start. It's always too soon to stop. Delayed obedience is disobedience. Obedience means at once. Many times we're not to understand, just obey. The quickest way to get out of the hole is to obey God. **There is a reason why God revealed the idea to you today.** "We ought to obey God rather than men" (Acts 5:29). Choosing to obey men is what keeps us from being instant to obey. Be instant to obey, taking action without delay. What most folks need is an alarm clock that will ring when it's time for them to rise to the occasion.

Why don't we jump at opportunities as quickly as we jump at conclusions? Procrastination is the grave in which opportunity is buried. **Anybody who brags about what he's going to do tomorrow probably did the same thing yesterday.** Few things are more dangerous to a person's character than having nothing to do and plenty of time in which to do it. Killing time is not murder, it's suicide. Two things rob people of their peace of mind: work unfinished and work not yet begun.

Opportunity is often lost in the deliberation. "Good resolutions are like babies crying in church; they should be carried out immediately," says Charles M. Sheldon. Tackle any difficulty at first sight, for the longer you gaze at it the bigger it becomes. The lazier a person is, the more he is going to do tomorrow. The tragedy of life is not that it ends so soon, but that we wait so long to begin it.

NUGGET #39

The Worst Buy Is An Alibi

Excuses are the nails used to build a house of failure. An alibi is worse and more terrible than a lie, for an alibi is a lie guarded. Ninety-nine percent of failures come from people who have the habit of making excuses. **When you're good at making excuses, it's hard to excel at anything else.** Don't make excuses, make progress. A person may fail many times, but he isn't a failure until he blames somebody or something else.

There may be many reasons for failure, but not a single excuse. Never let a challenge become an alibi. You have a choice: **You can let the obstacle be an alibi or an opportunity.** Excuses always replace progress. No alibi will ever serve the purpose of God.

An alibi is egotism wrong-side-out. Those who are unfaithful will always find an alibi. The person who really wants to do something finds a way; the other finds an excuse. Excuses always precipitate failure. "Bread of deceit is sweet to a man; but afterwards his mouth shall be filled with gravel" (Prov. 20:17).

It's been said that an excuse is a thin skin of falsehood stretched tightly over a bald-faced lie. **For every sin Satan is ready to provide an excuse.** Success is a matter of luck. Ask any failure. There are always enough excuses available if you are weak enough to use them. Don't buy that alibi.

NUGGET #40

Once You've Found A Better Way, Make That Way Better

All progress is due to those who were not satisfied to let well enough alone. "Acorns were good until bread was found," said Sir Francis Bacon. The majority of men meet with failure because of their lack of persistence in creating new plans to improve those that succeed.

If at first you do succeed, try something harder. There is no mistake so great as the mistake of quitting after a victory. If you can't think up a new idea, find a way to make better use of an old one. "Where we cannot invent, we may at least improve," said Charles Caleb Colton.

Don't look for the answer to your problem; look for many answers, then choose the best one. **The guy who moves ahead is the one who does more than is required and continues doing it.** "The difference between ordinary and extraordinary is that little extra," says Zig Ziglar.

There is always a way — there is always a better way. When you've found something — look again. School is never out! The more you truly desire something, the more you will try to find a better way.

The deeper we go in God, the deeper He goes in us. "A wise man will hear, and will increase learning" (Prov. 1:5).

The biggest enemy of best is good. If you're satisfied with what's good, you'll never have what's best. "It's what you learn after you know it all that counts," says John Wooden. **The man who thinks he knows it all has merely stopped thinking.** If you think you've arrived, you'll be left behind. A successful man continues to look for work after he has found a job.

Cause something to happen. "Show me a thoroughly satisfied man, and I will show you a failure," said Thomas Edison. "There are two kinds of men who never amount to very much," Cyrus H.K. Curtis remarked to his associate, Edward Bok. "And what kinds are those?" inquired Bok. "Those who cannot do what they are told," replied the famous publisher, "and those who can do nothing else." Find a better way, and make that way better.

PART II:
LOOKING OUTWARD

NUGGET #41

Say No To Many Good Ideas

One of the tricks of the devil is to get us to say yes to too many things. Then we end up being spread so thin that we are mediocre in everything and excellent in nothing.

There is one guaranteed formula for failure, and that is to try to please everyone.

There is a difference between something that is good and something that is right. Oftentimes, it is a challenge for many people to discern that which is good from that which is right. As Christians, our higher responsibility is always to do the right things. These come first. We should do the things that we're called to do, the things that are right, with excellence, first — before we start diversifying into other areas.

There comes a time in every person's life when he must learn to say no to many good ideas. In fact, the more an individual grows, the more opportunities he will have to say no. Becoming focused is a key to results. Perhaps no other virtue is so overlooked as a key to growth and success. The temptation is always to do a little bit of everything.

Saying no to a good idea doesn't always mean never. No may mean not right now.

There is power in the word *no*. No is an anointed word, one which can break the yoke of overcommitment and weakness. No can be used to turn a situation from bad to good, from wrong to right. Saying no can free you from burdens that you really don't need to carry right now.

It can also allow you to devote the correct amount of attention and effort to God's priorities in your life.

I'm sure that as you read the title of this nugget, past experiences and present situations come to mind. I'm sure you recall many situations in which no or not right now would have been the right answer. Don't put yourself through that kind of disappointment in the future.

Yes and no are the two most important words that you will ever say. These are the two words that determine your destiny in life. How and when you say them affects your entire future.

Saying no to lesser things can mean saying yes to the priorities in your life.

NUGGET #42

Your Best Friends Are Those Who Bring Out The Best In You

We need to be careful of the kind of insulation we use in our lives. We need to insulate ourselves from negative people and ideas. But, we should never insulate ourselves from godly counsel and wisdom.

It is a fact that misery wants your company. In Proverbs 27:19 (TLB) we read, *A mirror reflects a man's face, but what he is really like is shown by the kind of friends he chooses.* Proverbs 13:20 tells us, *He that walketh with wise men shall be wise: but a companion of fools shall be destroyed.* We become like those with whom we associate.

Some years ago I found myself at a stagnation point in my life. I was unproductive and unable to see clearly God's direction. One day I noticed that almost all of my friends were in the same situation. When we got together, all we talked about was our problems. As I prayed about this matter, God showed me that He desired that I have "foundational-level" people in my life. Such people who bring out the best in us, those who influence us to become better people ourselves. They cause us to have greater faith and confidence, to see things from God's perspectiv. After being with them, our spirits and our sights are raised.

I have found that **it is better to be alone than in the wrong company.** A single conversation with the right person can be more valuable than many years of study.

The Lord showed me that I needed to change my closest associations, and that there were some other people I needed to have contact with on a regular basis. These were men and women of great faith, those who made me a better person just by being around them. They were the ones who saw the gifts in me and could correct me in a constructive, loving way. My choice to change my closest associations was a turning point in my life.

When you surround yourself and affiliate with the right kind of people, you enter into the God-ordained power of agreement. Ecclesiastes 4:9,10,12 (TLB) states:

Two can accomplish more than twice as much as one, for the results can be much better. If one falls, the other pulls him up; but if a man falls when he is alone, he's in trouble.

And one standing alone can be attacked and defeated,but two can stand back-to-back and conquer; three is even better, for a triple-braided cord is not easily broken.

You need to steer clear of negative-thinking "experts." **Remember: in the eyes of average people average is always considered outstanding.** Look carefully at the closest associations in your life, for that is the direction you are heading.

NUGGET #43

Being A Servant Won't Make You Famous, Just Rich

Some time ago I received a telephone call. When I answered the phone, the voice on the other end of the line said: "Bang! You're dead!" I paused. I didn't quite know what to think about what had been said to me.

Then I heard a familiar voice, that of James Campbell, a client of mine: "John, just calling to remind you that we all need to die to ourselves every day."

That is true. There is always room at the top for anyone who is willing to say, "I'll serve."

Several years ago I was listening to Zig Ziglar. In his presentation, he said, "You'll always have everything in life that you want, if you'll help enough other people get what they want." When I heard that statement, something went off on the inside to me. Then and there I made a conscious decision to incorporate that concept into my life. It has made a tremendous difference.

True Christian leadership always begins with servanthood.

Selfishness always ends in self-destruction. John Ruskin said, "When a man is wrapped up in himself, he makes a pretty small package."

Being a servant is not always the most natural thing to do. You know, we are all conditioned to think about ourselves. That's why 97 percent of all people, when offered a new pen to try out, will write their own names. Yet despite our tendency toward self-promotion, it is always true that more is accomplished when nobody cares who gets the credit.

God has always called us to serve those whom we lead. Be willing to serve, without trying to reap the benefits. Before looking for a way to get, look for ways to give.

No one is truly a success in life until he has learned how to serve. The old saying is true: "The way to the throne room is through the servant's quarters." One of the most powerful decisions you can make in your life is to do something for someone who doesn't have the power or resources to return the favor. In Matthew 23:11 our Lord said: *...he that is greatest among you shall be your servant.* And in Matthew 20:26,27 He declared:

But it shall not be so among you: but whosoever will be great among you, let him be your minister;

And whosoever will be chief among you, let him be your servant.

One of the most incredible benefits of being a Christian is the fact that when you give of yourself to help other people, you cannot help but be personally and abundantly rewarded. The rewards and blessings of being a servant always extend far beyond what can be seen or heard.

NUGGET #44

We Are Called To Stand Out, Not Blend In

A majority, many times, is a group of highly motivated snails. If a thousand people say something foolish, it's still foolish. Truth is never dependent upon consensus of opinion.

In 1 Peter 2:9, the Bible says of us Christians, *...ye are a chosen generation, a royal priesthood, an holy nation, a peculiar people; that ye should shew forth the praises of him who hath called you out of darkness into his marvellous light.* Romans 12:2 exhorts us, *And be not conformed to this world, but be ye transformed by the renewing of your mind, that ye may prove what is that good, and acceptable, and perfect, will of God.*

One of the greatest compliments that anybody can give you is to say that you are different. We Christians live in this world, but we are aliens. We should talk differently, act differently, and perform differently. We are called to stand out.

There should be something different about you. If you don't stand out in a group, if there is not something unique or different in your life, you should re-evaluate yourself.

One way to stand head and shoulders above the crowd is to choose to do regular, ordinary things in an extraordinary and supernatural way with great enthusiasm. God has always done some of His very best work through remnants, when the circumstances appear to be stacked against them. In fact, in every battle described in the Bible, God was always on the side of the "underdog," the minority.

Majority rule is not always right. It is usually those people who don't have dreams or visions of their own who want to take a vote. People in groups tend to agree on courses of action that they as individuals know are not right.

Don't be persuaded or dissuaded by group opinion. It doesn't make any difference whether anyone else believes, you must believe. **Never take direction from a crowd for your personal life. And never choose to quit just because somebody else disagrees with you.** In fact, the two worst things you can say to yourself when you get an idea is: 1) "That has never been done before," and 2) "That has been done before." Just because somebody else has gone a particular way and not succeeded does not mean that you too will fail.

Be a pioneer, catch a few arrows, and stand out.

NUGGET #45

Expand Your Horizons

We all live under the same sky, but we don't all have the same horizon. Leaders always see a bigger picture. Expanding your horizons means being able to see the greater potential that's all around you.

The world's demands don't control the Christian's supply. "Don't be afraid to take a big step if one is indicated. You can't cross a chasm in two small jumps" (Unknown). "Aim at the sun and you may not reach it, but your arrow will fly far higher than if aimed at an object on a level with yourself," says Joel Hawes.

A woman's horizons were changed forever when she came up to Picasso in a restaurant and asked him to scribble something on her napkin. She said she'd be happy to pay him whatever he felt it was worth. Picasso did what she asked and then said, "That will be $10,000." "But you did that in only thirty seconds," the woman exclaimed. "No," Picasso said, "it has taken me forty years to do that."

"If the Son [of God] therefore shall make you free, ye shall be free indeed" (John 8:36). Knowing Jesus brings freedom, and freedom releases you to think and see higher. **Vision is the art of seeing things that are unseen.**

If what you did yesterday still looks big to you, you haven't done much today (The Sunday School). You will never learn faith in easy circumstances. **When God stretches you, you**

111

never snap back to your original shape. He who is afraid of doing too much always does too little. Make sure the road you're on is not leading to a cul-de-sac.

"Man cannot discover new oceans unless he has courage to lose sight of the shore" (Anonymous). That's why Jesus said, "Launch out into the deep!" (Luke 5:4) Enough spiritual power is going to waste to put Niagara Falls to shame. Unless you try to see beyond what you have already seen, you will never grow.

NUGGET #46

Today Is The Day To Decide To Go Through What You've Been Going Through

Stop talking constantly about the situation you are "going through." Decide today to get on through it! What do I mean by this statement? I mean, **don't accept your present, temporary situation as your future, permanent situation.** Despite your current circumstances, make up your mind to get on with your life and fulfill your divine purpose and calling.

God wants each of us to come through whatever situations we may face in life. We are not to be moved by what we see, but by what we do not see. This is what the Apostle Paul meant when he wrote that we walk by faith, not by sight. (2 Cor. 5:7.) Today is the day to begin to walk by faith — right out of your present circumstances!

If you have been saying for years, "I'm going through this situation," you need to change your story. Begin to declare: "I've had enough! Now is the time I'm going to get through this mess!"

The Bible contains many promises which can deliver you today. If you will believe and appropriate these promises, you will begin to see your circumstances line up with the Word and will of God — eventually, if not immediately.

You see, it's the devil who tells us that we will never be victorious, that we will never go through what we're going through. But in 1 Corinthians 10:13 (NIV) we are told, *No temptation has seized you except what is common to man. And God is faithful; he will not let you be tempted beyond what you can bear. But when you are tempted, he will also provide a way out so that you can stand up under it.*

This is your verse to take hold of and stand on. God is faithful. He will provide a way out. So you can take your stand of faith and boldly proclaim, "I'm going to go through with what I've been going through!" Natural circumstances may still remain unchanged, but between you and God, you are already through that situation.

Some people stay in the same hopeless situation their whole lives, never making a firm decision to seek God and His power to get through the circumstances they face. The commandment for us to be longsuffering does not require us to stay in a miserable situation one second longer than is absolutely necessary. Here's how we poise ourselves to break through: *And be not conformed to this world, but be ye transformed by the renewing of your mind, that ye may prove what is that good, and acceptable, and perfect, will of God* (Rom. 12:2). Be transformed by renewing your mind to the Word of God. Then you will know what is the good and perfect will of the Lord, and will be able to go through — once and for all —- what you've been going through so long.

NUGGET #47

You Were Created For Connection

God did not write solo parts for us. He has divine connections for you — the right friends and the right associations. These good connections always bring out the original in you. You know the kind of people I'm talking about. After you've been with them you find yourself less critical, more full of faith and with a vision for the future.

It is very important who we closely associate with. Have you ever known a backslider who didn't first hang around the wrong kind of people? The devil doesn't use strangers to deter or stop you. These wrong associations bring out the worst in you, not the best. After you're around them you'll find yourself full of doubt, fear, confusion and criticism.

As you grow in God your associations will change. Some of your friends will not want you to go on. They will want you to stay where they are. Friends who don't help you climb want you to crawl. **Your friends will stretch your vision or choke your dream.**

Never let anyone talk you out of pursuing a God-given idea. "Don't let someone else create your world for you, for when they do, they always make it too small," says men's minister Edwin Louis Cole. Who's creating your world? Never receive counsel from unproductive people. **Never discuss your**

problems with someone incapable of contributing to the solution. Those who never succeed themselves are always first to tell you how. Not everyone has a right to speak into your life. You are certain to get the worst of the bargain when you exchange ideas with a fool.

Don't follow anyone who's not going anywhere. We are to follow no person further than he or she follows Jesus. "When God gets ready to bless you, He brings a person into your life," says Mike Murdock. Respect those whom God has connected to you to help you. God cares for people through people.

With some people you spend an evening; with others you invest it. Be careful where you stop to inquire for directions along the road of life. Wise is the man who fortifies his life with the right friendships.

NUGGET #48

When You're Green With Envy, You're Ripe for Problems

One of the most valuable decisions we can make is not to compare our own lives with what is happening in other people's lives. What happens in someone else's life has nothing to do with what God is doing in yours. God loves you just as much as He loves others. "God is no respecter of persons" (Acts 10:34). **Every time we put our eyes on other people, we take our eyes off God.**

Some people seem to know how to live everybodys lives but their own. Envy is the consuming desire to have everybody else a little less successful than you are. Don't measure your success by what others haven't done. "Charity [love] envieth not" (1 Cor. 13:4). Jealousy is the tribute mediocrity pays to achievers. Criticizing another's garden doesn't keep the weeds out of your own.

Envy is a tremendous waste of mental energy. Refrain from it — it is the source of most unhappiness. If you're comparing yourself with others, your view is distorted. "Don't be content to be the chip off the old block, be the old block itself" (Winston Churchill). "Don't be a fraction, be a whole" (Greg Mason).

Don't surrender leadership of your destiny to outside forces. George Craig Stewart says, "Weak men are the slaves of what happens. Strong men are masters of what happens." The shoe doesn't tell the foot how big to grow. Having the right goals propels you to act from your vision and not from your circumstances.

Man is that foolish creature who tries to get even with his enemies and ahead of his friends. Love looks through a telescope; envy, through a microscope. We underrate or exaggerate that which we do not possess. Don't envy anybody. Every person possesses something no other person has. Develop that one thing and make it outstanding.

God enters by a private door into every individual. He leads each of us by a separate path. **No one can build his destiny upon the success of another person.** What the superior man seeks is in God; what the small man seeks is in others.

NUGGET #49

A Smile Is Mightier Than A Grin

The most bankrupt person in the world is the one who has lost his joy. A smile is the shortest distance between two people. Become the most positive and enthusiastic person you know.

In a recent survey two hundred national leaders were asked what makes a person successful. Eighty percent listed enthusiasm as the most important quality. Happiness is always an inside job. A person who is enthusiastic soon has enthusiastic followers. God's joy is contagious. "Keep your face to the sunshine and you cannot see the shadow," said Helen Keller.

How many people do you know who became successful doing something they hate? "Find something you love to do, and you'll never have to work another day in your life," says author Harvey Mackay.

The unwise person seeks happiness in the future; the wise person grows it today. **There is no sadder sight than a Christian pessimist.** Your world will look brighter from behind a smile.

Our first choice is to rejoice. "And we know that all that happens to us is working for our good if we love God and are fitting into his plans" (Rom. 8:28,TLB). Thomas Carlisle said, "Give me a man who sings at his work." That's the kind of people I want to hire! "Happy is that people, whose God is the Lord" (Ps. 144:15).

Greet the unseen with a cheer, not a fear. "Laughter is a form of internal jogging. It moves your internal organs around. It enhances respiration. It is an igniter of great expectations," says Norman Cousins. God says in His Word, "If you don't praise me, the rocks will." Let's not be replaced by a bunch of rocks!

Remember the steam kettle! Though up to its neck in hot water, it continues to sing. **For every minute you're angry, you lose sixty seconds of happiness.** Two things contribute to happiness: What we can do without, and what we can do with. People are about as happy as they make up their minds to be. Happiness can never be found, because it was never lost. A smile is mightier than a grin.

NUGGET #50

There Is Always Free Food On A Fish Hook

Did you know that the best shortcut you can ever take is to do what God says, in His timing? Shortcuts outside of the will of God invite compromise and create strife and confusion.

We believers need to understand that we are long- distance runners. We are marathoners. We are not on a sprint. We do not need to look for get-rich-quick schemes or shortcuts that open the door to compromise.

There is an old saying that is absolutely true: "If you keep your attention on learning the tricks of the trade, you will never learn the trade." Watch out for fads, even spiritual fads because the letters of the word fad stand for "For A Day."

There is a story told of a beautiful bird that was known for its great singing. It would sit at the top of a tree and make all kinds of lovely melodies. One day a man was walking through the woods. He passed by the tree and heard this beautiful bird singing. The bird saw the man and perceived that he was holding a box.

"What do you have in the box?" he asked the man.

The man replied that he had large, juicy earthworms in the box. "I will sell you a worm for one of your beautiful feathers," he offered.

121

The bird reached down, pulled out a feather, and gave it in exchange for a worm. Then he took the worm and ate it. He reflected to himself, "Why should I have to work so hard to get a worm when it's so easy to get one this way?"

Well, this affair continued over a period of many days and soon the bird no longer had any beautiful feathers to use to pay for worms. Furthermore, he could no longer fly, nor was he pretty any longer. So he didn't feel like singing beautiful songs any more. He was a very unwise and unhappy bird.

Like this foolish bird, we are always subject to the temptation to look for shortcuts, ways to get ahead and obtain the things we want and the results we desire. But, as this poor creature learned to his regret, there is a price associated with taking shortcuts.

Eventually, we will learn that there is no shortcut to success. One of the hidden truths of life is the fact that the path to the prize is always more valuable than the prize itself. Shortcuts rob us of those valuable lessons that we need to learn along the way. When presented with an option of a shortcut, a way that is not of God, say no. Be persistent and stick to the path on which the Lord has placed you.

Yes, it's true: **we must stay on the path of the circumference of time before we arrive at the center of opportunity.**

NUGGET #51

If You Pluck The Blossoms, You Must Do Without The Fruit

God is a God of seasons. "To every thing there is a season, and a time to every purpose under the heaven," says Ecclesiastes 3:1. Distinctly different things happen during different seasons. There is a wintertime in God. It is a season of preparation, revelation and direction. It is also the time when the roots grow. God wants to establish the right foundation in you during this season. But there is no harvest now.

There is a springtime in God. It is a time of planting, hoeing and nurturing. In other words, hard work. God wants you to work your plan. But there is no harvest in springtime.

There is a summertime in God. Summer is a time of great growth. Now is the time when activity, interest and people begin to surround your God-given idea. For all the activity of summer, there is only a minimal harvest. But then comes autumn.

This is God's harvest time. It is during this season that the harvest is reaped in much greater proportion than the work, activity or idea expended. But most people never make it to the fall. Often, they end up quitting along the way because they don't know what season they're in.

When you understand that God is a God of seasons, it prepares you to do the right thing at the right time. It inspires you to persevere to the fall. God's Word is true when it says, "Let us not become weary in doing good, for at the proper time we will reap a harvest if we do not give up" (Gal. 6:9, NIV).

It was spring, but it was summer I wanted,
the warm days, and the great outdoors.
It was summer, but it was fall I wanted,
the colorful leaves, and the cool, dry air.
It was spring, but it was winter I wanted,
the beautiful snow, and the joy of the holiday season.
I was a child, but it was adulthood I wanted,
the freedom, and the respect.
I was twenty, but it was thirty I wanted,
to be mature, and sophisticated.
I was middle-aged, but it was thirty I wanted,
the youth, and the free spirit.
I was retired, but it was middle age I wanted,
the presence of mind, without limitations.
My life was over,
but I never got what I wanted.

—Jason Lehman

If you pluck the blossoms, you must do without the fruit.

NUGGET #52

There Are No Unimportant People

You are not insignificant. Never view your life as if Jesus did nothing for you. Make the most of yourself, for that is all that God made of you. The first and worst of all frauds is to betray yourself. If you deliberately plan to be less than you are capable of being, you will bring unhappiness to the rest of your life.

Too many people never begin to do what God wants them to do because they are waiting to be able to sing like Sandi Patti, preach like Billy Graham or write like Chuck Swindoll before they start. God knew what He was doing when He put you together. Use what talents you possess. The woods would be very silent if the only birds that sang were those that sang the very best.

You were created for achievement. You have been given the seeds for greatness. What is greatness? What is achievement? It is doing what God wants you to do and being where He wants you to be.

Christians are new creations, not rebuilt sinners. Don't ever forget that God calls you a friend (see John 15:15). What an incredible statement that is! He also says you are "wonderfully made" (Ps. 139:14).

You're beginning to see that God made you special for a purpose. He has a job for you that no one else can do as well

as you. Out of the billions of applicants, only one is qualified, only one has the right combination of what it takes. God has given each person the measure of faith to do what He has called them to do. Every person is gifted.

A person is never what he ought to be until he is doing what he ought to be doing. God holds us not only responsible for what we have, but for what we could have; not only for what we are, but for what we might be. Man is responsible to God for becoming what God has made possible for him to become.

Your life makes a difference. Although we're all different, no mixture is insignificant. On judgment day, God won't ask me why I wasn't Joshua or Billy Graham or Pat Robertson but why I wasn't John Mason. Jerry Van Dyke said it best when he said, "The best rose bush is not the one with the fewest thorns, but that which bears the finest roses."

NUGGET #53

When You Refuse To Change, You End Up In Chains

We humans are custom-built for change.

Inanimate objects like clothes, houses, and buildings don't have the ability to truly change. They grow out of style and become unusable. But at any point in time, at any age, any one of us is able to change. To change doesn't always mean to do the opposite. In fact, most of the time, it means to add on to or slightly adjust.

When we are called upon by the Lord to change, we will continue to reach toward the same goal, but perhaps in a slightly different way. When we refuse to cooperate with the change that God is requiring of us, we make chains that constrain and restrict us.

There are three things that we know about the future: 1) it is not going to be like the past, 2) it is not going to be exactly the way we think it's going to be, and 3) the rate of change will take place faster than we imagine. The Bible indicates that in the end times in which we are now living, changes will come about much quicker than ever before in history.

In 1803 the British created a civil service position in which a man was required to stand on the cliffs of Dover with a spy

127

glass. His job was to be on the lookout for invasion. He was to ring a bell if he saw the army of Napoleon Bonaparte approaching. Now that was all well and good for the time, but that job was not eliminated until 1945! How many spy glasses on the cliffs of Dover are we still holding onto in our lives? **We should choose not to allow "the way we've always done it" to cause us to miss opportunities God is providing for us today.**

Even the most precious of all gems needs to be chiseled and faceted to achieve its best luster. There is nothing that remains so constant as change. Don't end up like concrete, all mixed up and permanently set.

In Isaiah 42:9, the Lord declares: *Behold, the former things are come to pass, and new things do I declare: before they spring forth I tell you of them.* The Bible is a book that tells us how to respond to change ahead of time. You see, I believe that we can decide in advance how we will respond to most situations. When I was coaching basketball many years ago, I used to tell my players that most situations in a game can be prepared for ahead of time. We used to practice different game situations so that when the players got into an actual game situation they would know how to respond. **One of the main reasons the Bible was written was to prepare us ahead of time, to teach us how to respond in advance to many of the situations that we will encounter in life.**

Choose to flow with God's plan. Be sensitive to the new things He is doing. Stay flexible to the Holy Spirit and know that ours is a God who directs, adjusts, moves, and corrects us. He is always working to bring us into perfection.

NUGGET #54

Everything Big Starts With Something Little

All of God's great people in the Bible were faithful in the small things. In Matthew 25 Jesus told the parable of the talents. In it He referred to the one servant who had taken his master's money and multiplied it. In verse 23 his master said to that man, ...*Well done, good and faithful servant; thou hast been faithful over a few things, I will make thee ruler over many things: enter thou into the joy of thy lord.* In Zechariah 4:10 the Lord asks the prophet, *For who hath despised the day of small things?*.... There is a powerful principle in taking small steps.

Many people are not moving with God today simply because they were not willing to take the small steps He placed before them. If you have received a call into any particular area, you should leap at the opportunity — no matter how small — to move in the direction in which the Lord has called you. If you are called to be a youth pastor, and are sitting at home waiting for an invitation from some large church, you should know that it will never come. You need to find the first young person you can, put your arm around him, and begin to minister to him.

Don't be afraid to take small steps. The Bible promises us that if we are faithful in small matters, one day we will be rulers over many larger things.

The impossible, many times, is just simply the untried.

I can remember a time in my life when I was literally frozen with fear at what God had called me to do. It seemed so huge a task that I was unable to bring myself to face it. A friend came to me and spoke two words that broke that paralysis in my life. He said simply, "Do something!" If you are at a point of paralysis in your life because of what God wants you to do, the word for you today is "Do something!" Don't worry about the goal, just take the steps that take you past the starting point and soon you'll get to a point of no return. As you climb higher, you'll be able to see much farther.

We should all learn to grow wherever we're planted.

As you begin, don't be afraid. Eric Hoffer said: "Fear of becoming a has-been keeps some people from becoming anything." Every great idea is impossible from where you are starting today. But little goals add up, and they add up rapidly. Most people don't succeed because they are too afraid even to try. They don't begin because of that old fear of failure.

Many times the final goal seems so unreachable that it keeps us from even making an effort. But, once you've made your decision and have started, you are more than half-way there. God will begin with you today — no matter what your circumstances. Just think how thankful you would be if you lost everything you have right now and then got it all back again. Wouldn't you be ready to go? Choose to think eternally, but act daily.

NUGGET #55

A Chip On The Shoulder Weighs A Ton

Forgiveness is essential for good human relationships. You cannot give a hug with your arms folded.

Forgiveness of others also assures us of God's forgiveness of our own faults and failures. In Matthew 6:14,15 (NIV) Jesus said, *"For if you forgive men when they sin against you, your heavenly Father will also forgive you. But if you do not forgive men their sins, your Father will not forgive your sins."* The weight of unforgiveness greatly drags a person down. It is a tremendous load to carry in the race that we Christians are called to run.

When faced with the decision to forgive and forget, never make the excuse, "But no one knows what that person did to me!" That may be true, but the question is: do you know what unforgiveness will do to you?

What really matters is what happens in us not to us.

Unforgiveness leads to great bitterness, which is a deadly misuse of the creative flow from above. Great amounts of mental energy and brain power are used up in pondering over a negative situation and plotting how to "get even." This kind of thinking is totally unproductive. People who make a habit of burning bridges will discover that it is they who have been left isolated and alone and that they will deal with neutrals and enemies the rest of their lives. That's why we should build bridges, not burn them. Vengeance is a poor traveling companion. Every Christian is called to a ministry of reconciliation. (2 Cor. 5:18.) Getting even always causes imbalance and unhappiness in a life.

As I have worked with churches throughout America, in every stagnating situation I have found areas of unforgiveness. And conversely, I have found that, generally speaking, churches which are growing don't talk about past problems.

Never underestimate the power of forgiveness to loose and free you to accomplish your goals and fulfill your calling. It is the one power you have over a person who slanders or criticizes you. **The farther you walk in forgiveness, the greater the distance you put between yourself and the negative situation.**

Forgiveness gives you a spring in your spiritual walk and a second wind in the race of life.

NUGGET #56

The Doors of Opportunity Are Marked "Push"

Get aggressive and go after opportunities. They may not find you. **The reason some people don't go very far in life is because they sidestep opportunity and shake hands with procrastination.** Procrastination is the grave in which opportunity is buried. Don't be out in the backyard looking for four-leaf clovers when opportunity knocks at your front door. For the tenacious there is always time and opportunity.

Watch for big problems; they disguise big opportunities. Opposition, distraction and challenges always surround the birth of a dream. Make the most of all that comes and the least of all that goes. **Adversity is fertile soil for creativity.**

To the alert Christian, interruptions are only divinely inserted opportunities. Life's disappointments are love's hidden appointments. When God prepares to do something wonderful, He begins with a difficulty. When He plans to do something very wonderful, He begins with an impossibility!

"A wise man will make more opportunities than he finds," said Francis Bacon. It's more valuable to find a situation that redistributes opportunity than one that redistributes wealth. Have you ever noticed that great people are never lacking for opportunities? When successful people are interviewed, they always mention their big plans for the future when most of us would think, "If I were in their shoes, I'd kick back and do nothing." Success doesn't diminish their dreams.

There is far more opportunity than ability. Life is full of golden opportunities for doing what we are called to do. Every person has a lot that he can do. Start with what you can do; don't stop because of what you can't do. Great opportunities come to those who make the most of small ones. Many people seem to think that opportunity means a chance to get money without earning it. **God's best gifts to us are not things, but opportunities.** And those doors of opportunity are marked "push."

NUGGET #57

Leave Everyone a Little Better Than You Found Them

Proverbs 11:24,25 (TLB) says, "It is possible to give away and become richer! It is also possible to hold on too tightly and lose everything. Yes, the liberal man shall be rich! By watering others, he waters himself. You were created to help others."

If you treat a person as he is, he will remain as he is. If you treat him as if he were what he could be, he will become what he could be. There is no exercise better for the heart than reaching down and lifting someone else up.

An optimist is always able to see the bright side of other people's troubles. **Practicing the Golden Rule is not a sacrifice, it's an investment.** Don't give till it hurts, give till it feels good.

What we do for ourselves alone dies with us; what we do for others is timeless. No man is more deceived than the selfish man. "No man was ever honored for what he received. Honor has been the reward for what he gave," said Calvin Coolidge. Invest in the success of others. **When you help someone up a mountain, you'll find yourself close to the summit too.**

If you want others to improve, let them hear the nice things you say about them. People will treat you the way you view them. Find the good in everyone. Draw out their gifts and callings. To lead people, make them feel you are behind them. Most people can smile for two months on five words of praise and a pat on the back.

What good thing you make come to pass for others, God will make come to pass for you. "Knowing that whatsoever good thing any man doeth, the same shall he receive of the Lord" (Eph. 6:8). You grow spiritually to the extent that you give out. By giving out, you create more room to grow on the inside.

"Give instruction to a wise man, and he will be yet wiser: teach a just man, and he will increase in learning" (Prov. 9:9). What I gave, I have; what I spent, I had; what I kept, I lost (Old epitaph). No man is more deceived than the selfish man. You may be the only Bible some people will ever read. Remember the words of D. L. Moody: "Where one reads the Bible, a hundred read you and me."

What means most in life is what you have done for others. The best way to encourage yourself is to encourage someone else. It is the duty of all Christians to make it difficult for others to do wrong, easy to do right. "Those who bring sunshine to the lives of others cannot keep it from themselves," said James Matthew Barrie.

NUGGET #58

Never Surrender Your Dream To Noisy Negatives

Nobody can ever make you feel average without your permission. Ingratitude and criticism are going to come; they are a part of the price paid for leaping past mediocrity.

Jesus Himself, after healing the ten lepers, was only thanked by one of them. (Luke 17:11-19.) Instead of being surprised by ingratitude from others, we should learn to expect it.

If you move with God, you will be criticized. **The only sure way to fend off criticism is to do nothing and be nothing.** Those who do things inevitably stir up criticism.

But the Bible offers this great promise concerning criticism: **the truth always outlives a lie.** This fact is backed up by Proverbs 12:19: *The lip of truth shall be established for ever: but a lying tongue is but for a moment.* Also, in Hebrews 13:6 we are told ...*that we may boldly say, The Lord is my helper, and I will not fear what man shall do unto me.*

We should never judge a person by what is said of him by his enemies. Kenneth Tynan has provided the best description of a critic I have ever heard. "A critic," he said, "is a man who knows the way but can't drive the car." **We Christians are not called to respond to criticism; we are called to respond to God.**

Often, criticism will present the best platform from which to proclaim the truth.

Most of the time people who are critical are either jealous or uninformed. They usually say things that have no impact whatsoever upon the truth. There's a famous anonymous saying that describes this situation perfectly: "It is useless for the sheep to pass resolutions in favor of vegetarianism while the wolf remains of a different opinion." If what you say and do is of God, it will not make any difference if every person on the face of the earth stands up and criticizes. Likewise, if it is not of God, nothing other people say will make it right.

Pay no attention to negative criticism. *Trust in the Lord, and do good...*(Ps. 37:3) knowing that in the end what you do in the Lord will be rewarded.

NUGGET #59

Your Problem Is
Your Promotion

Every obstacle introduces a person to himself.

How we respond to obstacles in our path is important.

The greatest example of an obstacle in the Bible is the giant Goliath who confronted and intimidated the armies of Israel, including the brothers of a young shepherd lad man named David. Of course, we know that David's brothers chose not to do anything about the obstacle before them, but David did. The difference between David and his brothers was this: the brothers looked at the obstacle and figured it was too big to hit, but David looked at the obstacle and figured it was too big to miss.

The way you look at any obstacle in your life makes all the difference.

Let each new obstacle force you to go to the next level in God. **No obstacle will ever leave you the way it found you.** You will either be better or you will be worse as a result of that confrontation.

But keep in mind one important fact about obstacles: every obstacle has a limited lifespan. Many times there are things that we worried about last year that we can't even remember today. One of the biggest lies of the devil is that things will not change, that they will not pass.

Mediocre people tend to be tamed and subdued by obstacles, but great leaders always rise above them. You and I need to be like the great man, who, when asked what helped him overcome the obstacles of life, responded, "The other obstacles." We should be like a kite that rises against the wind, causing it to mount higher and higher. Every problem has a soft spot — there is an answer.

Since many of the obstacles we face are money related, the correct perspective is to know that if a problem can be solved with a checkbook, it's not really an obstacle; it's an expense.

Someone has said that obstacles are what we see when we take our eyes off the goal. Keep your eyes on the goal and remember that you are not alone in your struggle for *...we know that in all things God works for the good of those who love him, who have been called according to his purpose* (Rom. 8:28 NIV).

Really, **in times of adversity you don't have an obstacle to deal with, you have a choice to make.** In the midst of unbelievable circumstances, believe.

NUGGET #60

If In Doubt, Don't

One day a hunter came across a bear in the woods. The bear said to the hunter, "I want a full stomach."

The hunter responded, "I want a fur coat."

"Let's compromise," suggested the bear — and promptly ate the man. As a result, they both got what they wanted. The bear went away with a full stomach and the man went away wrapped in fur.

This hunter learned the lesson of compromise: **when having to choose between the lesser of two evils, choose neither.**

In Deuteronomy 30:19 (NIV) the Lord says to His people, *This day I call heaven and earth as witnesses against you that I have set before you life and death, blessings and curses. Now choose life, so that you and your children may live.* You and I have a choice. Every day we must choose between life and death. We should never settle for just anything; we should always seek the best. The fact is that it is rarely the strong man who urges compromise. A compromise will always be more expensive than either of the alternatives.

The call of God is always a call to excellence — never a call to mediocrity. If anything is worth doing at all, it is worth doing well. If you can't do it with excellence, don't bother.

Someone has said, "If you don't have time to do it right, when will you have time to do it over?"

When compromise is allowed in one area, it always leaks out and begins to affect other areas. It also allows lies, deceit, and error to creep into a life and take it over. I know people who have turned from the Lord completely. Their troubles all started because of compromises at work. They began to give in on little things, which soon became bigger things. It wasn't long before compromise had begun to infiltrate their personal life, then their home life. Eventually it overtook and overwhelmed them.

In Proverbs 4:26,27, the writer warns us:

Ponder the path of thy feet, and let all thy ways be established.

Turn not to the right hand nor to the left: remove thy foot from evil.

Don't allow compromise to creep in and destroy. You can't say, "Well, I'll compromise in this one area and everything else will be okay." Once it has a foothold, compromise grows and spreads.

Be a person of integrity. Guard your reputation, and the reputation of Jesus Christ and His Church. If the only way others can tell that you are a Christian is by the symbol of the fish on your business card, do us all a favor and leave it off. Take a stand today against compromise.

NUGGET #61

There Is No Such Thing As A Self-Made Man

No one makes it alone. Have a grateful heart and be quick to acknowledge those who help you. Remember, if you try to go it alone, then the fence that shuts others out shuts you in. **"God sends no one away except those who are full of themselves"** (D.L. Moody). The man who only works by himself and for himself is likely to be corrupted by the company he keeps.

"Everyone who has ever done a kind deed for us, or spoken one word of encouragement to us, has entered into the make-up of our character and of our thoughts, as well as our success," says George Matthew Adams. Make yourself indispensable to somebody. It is easy to blame others for your failures, but do you credit others with your successes?

Work together with others. Remember the banana: Every time it leaves the bunch, it gets peeled and eaten. You'll never experience lasting success without relationships with people. No one person alone can match the cooperative effort of the right team. **"We" makes "me" stronger.**

"Tunnel vision tells you nobody is working as hard as you are. Tunnel vision is an enemy of teamwork. Tunnel vision is a door through which division and strife enter" (Tim Redmond). Few burdens are heavy when everybody lifts. Freckles would make a nice tan if they would get together.

The man who believes in nothing but himself lives in a very small world — one in which few will want to enter. The man who sings his own praises may have the right tune but the wrong lyrics. **The higher you go in life, the more dependent you become on other people.** A conceited person never gets anywhere because he thinks he is already there.

NUGGET #62

"An Army Of Sheep Led By A Lion Would Defeat An Army Of Lions Led By A Sheep"
– Old Arab Proverb

What are the actions and attributes of a leader? What is it that makes him different from others?

1. A leader is always full of praise.

2. A leader learns to use the phrases "thank you" and "please" on his way to the top.

3. A leader is always growing.

4. A leader is possessed with his dreams.

5. A leader launches forth before success is certain.

6. A leader is not afraid of confrontation.

7. A leader talks about his own mistakes before talking about someone else's.

8. A leader is a person of honesty and integrity.

9. A leader has a good name.

145

10. A leader makes others better.

11. A leader is quick to praise and encourage the smallest amount of improvement.

12. A leader is genuinely interested in others.

13. A leader looks for opportunities to find someone doing something right.

14. A leader takes others up with him.

15. A leader responds to his own failures and acknowledges them before others have to discover and reveal them.

16. A leader never allows murmuring — from himself or others.

17. A leader is specific in what he expects.

18. A leaders holds accountable those who work with him.

19. A leader does what is right rather than what is popular.

20. A leader is a servant.

A leader is a lion, not a sheep.

NUGGET #63

Words Are Like Nitroglycerine: They Can Blow Up Bridges or Heal Hearts

Just to see how it feels, for the next twenty-four hours refrain from saying anything bad about anyone or anything. "The difference between the right word and the almost right word is the difference between lightning and the lightning bug," said Mark Twain. Proverbs 16:27 (TLB) says, "*Idle hands are the devil's workshop; idle lips are his mouthpiece. "It is true that death and life are in the power of the tongue*" (Prov 18:21).

You can tell more about a person by what he says about others than by what others say about him. Jesus said, "*Out of the abundance of the heart the mouth speaketh*" (Matt. 12:34). An original person says, "Let's find a way"; a copy says, "There is no way." An original says, "There should be a better way to do it"; a copy says, "That's the way it's always been done." Instead of using the words "if only," try substituting "next time." Don't ask, "What if it doesn't work?" Ask instead, "What if it does?"

Ignorance is always eager to speak. The best time to hold your tongue is when you feel you must say something. You'll never be hurt by anything you didn't say. Silence is the ultimate weapon of power; it is also one of the hardest arguments to dispute. Never judge a person's horsepower by his exhaust.

Some people speak from experience; others, from experience, don't speak.

Take a tip from nature — your ears aren't made to shut, but your mouth is! When an argument flares up, the wise man quenches it with silence. Sometimes you have to be quiet to be heard. It's when the fish opens his mouth that he gets caught.

Your words are a reflection of your destiny. Jesus said, "Your words now reflect your fate then: either you will be justified by them or you will be condemned" (Matt. 12:37, TLB). The book of Exodus says, "*Now go ahead and do as I [the Lord] tell you, for I will help you to speak well, and I will tell you what to say*" (Ex. 4:12 TLB).

To know a man, listen carefully when he mentions his dislikes. Flapping gums dull your two most important senses—your sight and sound. Many a great idea has been quenched by wrong words. **Know that every time you say "God" you say "miracle."**

A wise old owl sat on an oak,
The more he saw the less he spoke;
The less he spoke the more he heard;
Why aren't we like that wise old bird?
                              —Edward H. Richards

NUGGET #64

Making Others Better
Is A Boomerang

A famous old poem goes like this:

"When days are hot and flies are thick, use horse sense — cooperate.

This is a truth all horses know, they learned it many centuries ago.

One tail on duty at the rear can reach that fly behind the ear.

But two tails when arranged with proper craft can do the job both fore and aft."

Your decision to bound past mediocrity will help pull up others with you.

Choosing God's will in our lives always affects others and makes them better. William Danforth said, "Our most valuable possessions are those which can be shared without lessening those which when shared multiply. Our least valuable possessions are those which when divided are diminished."

We should look for opportunities to invest of ourselves in others and to help make them better.

Somebody did that for you once. Somebody saw something in you and reached out to help you. That act of kindness has determined where you are today. It may have been your pastor, your parents, a friend, a teacher, coach, neighbor, or just someone who offered some extra money, prayers, good advice, or equipment and supplies. But whoever it was, that individual had the foresight and the resources to invest in you and take a risk on your future.

I have a challenge for you. This week take a few minutes and send a note to those people who reached out and greatly affected your life. Also do this: take a few minutes and reach out to help someone else get ahead. You will find that this will be one of the most satisfying experiences you've had in a long time.

Proverbs 3:27 says, *Withhold not good from them to whom it is due, when it is in the power of thine hand to do it.* Invest in somebody today. Believe in that person. Offer support and encouragement. Help him come up to another level.

Try it, you'll like it! You'll also benefit from it!

NUGGET #65

People Are Born Originals, But Most Die Copies

The call in your life is not a copy.

In this day of peer pressure, trends, and fads, we need to realize and accept that each person has been custom-made by God the Creator. Each of us has a unique and personal call upon our lives. We are to be our own selves and not copy other people.

Because I do a lot of work with churches, I come into contact with many different types of people. One time I talked over the phone with a pastor I had never met and who did not know me personally. We came to an agreement that I was to visit his church as a consultant. As we were closing our conversation and were setting a time to meet at the local airport, he asked me, "How will I know you when you get off the plane?"

"Oh, don't worry, pastor; I'll know you," I responded jokingly. "You all look alike."

The point of this humorous story is this: **be the person God has made YOU to be.**

The call of God upon our lives is the provision of God in our lives. We do not need to come up to the standards of anyone else. **The average person compares himself with others, but we Christians should always compare ourselves with the person God has called us to be.** That is our standard — God's unique plan and design for our lives. How the Lord chooses to deal with others has nothing to do with our individual call in life or God's timing and direction for us.

You and I can always find someone richer than we are, poorer than we are, or with more or less ability than we have. But how other people are, what they have, and what happens in their lives, has no effect upon our call. In Galatians 6:4 (TLB) we are admonished: *Let everyone be sure that he is doing his very best, for then he will have the personal satisfaction of work well done, and won't need to compare himself with someone else.*

God made you a certain way. You are unique. You are one of a kind. To copy others is to cheat yourself out of the fullness of what God has called you to be and to do.

So, choose to accept and become the person God has made you to be. Tap into the originality and creative genius of God in your life.

NUGGET #66

Go Out On A Limb – That's Where the Fruit Is

Be bold and courageous. When you look back on your life, you'll regret the things you didn't do more than the things you did. When facing a difficult task, act as though it is impossible to fail. If you're going to climb Mount Everest, bring along the American flag. Go from looking at what you can see to believing what you can have. **Don't undertake a plan unless it is distinctly important and nearly impossible.** Don't bunt — aim out of the ballpark.

The mediocre man thinks he isn't. "Not doing more than the average is what keeps the average down," says William M. Winans. "Undertake something that is difficult; it will do you good. Unless you try to do something beyond what you have already mastered, you will never grow," said Ronald E. Osborn. It is difficult to say what is truly impossible, for what we take for granted today seemed impossible yesterday. "Impossible," Napoleon is quoted as saying, "is a word found only in the dictionary of fools." What words are found in your dictionary?

He who is afraid of doing too much always does too little. To achieve all that is possible, we must attempt the impossible. Your vision becomes your potential worth. **Learn to be comfortable with great dreams.**

The best jobs haven't been found. The best work hasn't been done. Don't listen to those who say, "It's not done that way." Don't listen to those who say, "You're taking too big a chance." If Michelangelo had painted the floor of the Sistine Chapel, it would surely be rubbed out by today. "Always aim high, going after things that will make a difference rather than seeking the safe path of mediocrity," says Wess Roberts.

Don't bother with small plans, for they motivate no one. After Roger Bannister broke the four-minute mile, within one year thirty-seven others broke it; within two years three hundred had broken it. Thinking high affects others.

The readiness to take risks is our grasp of faith. God puts no restriction on faith; faith puts no restriction on God. "*But without faith it is impossible to please him*" (Heb. 11:6). Your vision must be bigger than you. Let us say, "*Lead me to the rock that is higher than I*" (Ps. 61:2).

Christians are not to stay in the shadow but to stretch in the light of the Cross. He who expects nothing shall never be disappointed. "*Is any thing too hard for the Lord?*" (Gen. 18:14).

"Don't avoid extremes to stay 'in balance', stay in balance by living in the extreme that God wills at that time in your life," says Tim Redmond. Unless a man takes on more than he can possibly do, he will never do all that he can. "Brethren, be great believers. Little faith will bring your souls to heaven, but great faith will bring heaven to your souls," said Charles Spurgeon.

The most disappointed people in the world are those who get just what is coming to them and no more. **There are a lot of ways to become a failure, but never taking a chance is the most successful.** Some things have to be believed to be seen. Attempt something so fantastic that unless God is in it, it is destined for failure.

NUGGET #67

Decision Determines Destiny

The Bible says that a double-minded man is unstable in all his ways. I know people who are triple-minded...I don't know what they are. It's not the difference between people that's the difficulty, it's the indifference. All around us, fools seem to be growing without watering. **Too many people spend their lives failing and never even notice.**

God wants us to be the most decisive people on the face of the earth. Why did He give us His Word and the Holy Spirit? So that we can live decisive lives! How can the Lord guide a man if he hasn't made up his mind which way he wants to go? All of us are at fault for all of the good we didn't do. "The average man does not know what to do with this life, yet wants another one which will last forever," said Anatold France.

The most unhappy people are those who can never make a decision. An indecisive person can never be said to belong to himself. **Don't worry about not making a decision; someone else will make it for you.** You can't grow while letting others make decisions for you. Indecisive people are like a blind man looking in a dark room for a black cat that isn't there.

The devil is the only one who can use a neutral person. Jesus said in Matthew 12:30 (NIV), *"He who is not with me is against me, and he who does not gather with me scatters."* Making no decision is a decision. It does not require a decision to go to hell. "Mistrust the man who finds everything good, the man who finds everything evil and, still more, the man who is indifferent to everything," says Larry Bielat.

As you are reading this, think of one decision you need to make. Meet the little problems and opportunities of your life with decision. **A great deal of talent is lost for want of a little decision.** "Decision is a sharp knife that cuts clean and straight; indecision is a dull one that hacks and tears and leaves ragged edges behind," says Gordon Graham.

Faith demands a decision before it can work. Every accomplishment great or small starts with a decision. Not everything that is met can be changed, but nothing can be changed until it is met. "*If ye will not believe, surely ye shall not be established*" (Is. 7:9). "*If the trumpet give an uncertain sound, who shall prepare himself to the battle?*" (1 Cor. 14:8).

Remain indecisive, and you will never grow. To move on from where you are, decide where you would rather be. Decision determines destiny.

NUGGET #68

You Can't Walk Backward Into The Future

It is more valuable to look where you're going than to see where you've been. Don't see your future only from the perspective of yesterday. It's too easy to quantify and qualify everything and choke off the dream within you. "The past should be a springboard, not a hammock," said Edmund Burke. You can never plan the future by the past. No one can walk backward into the future. **Those to whom yesterday still looks big aren't doing much today.**

Your future contains more happiness than any past you can remember. "The born-again Christian has no past," says Tim Redmond. Second Corinthians 5:17 (NIV) says, *"Therefore, if anyone is in Christ, he is a new creation; the old has gone, the new has come!"* God doesn't look at your past to decide your future.

"Misery is a yesterday person trying to get along with a tomorrow God," says Mike Murdock. Don't let your past mistakes become memorials. They should be cremated, not embalmed. It is important to look forward — your calling and destiny are there. The apostle Paul said, *"Forgetting what is behind and straining toward what is ahead, I press on toward the goal to win the prize for which God has called me heavenward in Christ Jesus"* (Phil. 3:13,14, NIV).

Those who predominantly talk about the past are going backward. Those who talk about the present are just maintaining. But those who talk about the future are growing.

Some people stay so far in the past that the future is gone before they get there. The future frightens only those who prefer living in the past. No one has ever backed into prosperity. You can't have a better tomorrow if you are thinking about yesterday today. Yesterday has passed forever and is beyond our control. What lies behind us is insignificant compared to what lies ahead.

NUGGET #69

One Action Is More Valuable Than a Thousand Good Intentions

"As He [Jesus] was speaking, a woman in the crowd called out, 'God bless your mother — the womb from which you came, and the breasts that gave you suck!' He replied, 'Yes, but even more blessed are all who hear the Word of God and put it into practice" (Luke 11:27, 28 TLB). It is more blessed to be a doer of the Word of God than even to have been the mother of Jesus.

Few dreams come true by themselves. The test of a person lies in action. **No one ever stumbled onto something big while sitting down.** Even a fly doesn't get a slap on the back until he starts to work. A famous poem by an unknown author states, "Sitting still and wishing makes no person great; the good Lord sends the fishing, but you must dig the bait."

Realize that nothing is learned while you talk. Words without actions are the assassins of dreams. The smallest good deed is better than the greatest intention. History is made whenever you take the right action. Action is the proper fruit of knowledge. Getting an idea should be like sitting on a tack — it should make you jump up and do something.

"Go to the ant, thou sluggard; consider her ways, and be wise: which having no guide, overseer, or ruler, provideth her meat in the summer, and gathereth her food in the harvest"

(Prov. 6:6-8). "Nothing preaches better than this ant, yet she says nothing" (Ben Franklin). You earn respect only by action; inaction earns disrespect.

Some people find life an empty dream because they put nothing into it. Every time one person expresses an idea, he finds ten others who thought of it before — but took no action. Mark Twain said, "Thunder is good, thunder is impressive, but it is lightning that does the work." The test of this book is that the reader goes away saying, not "What a lovely book" but, "I will do something!"

The devil is willing for you to confess faith as long as you don't practice it. When praying, we must simultaneously be willing to take the action that God directs in the answer to our prayer. The answers to your prayers will include action.

The Bible tells us that action gives life to faith (see James 2:26). *"Even a child is known by his doings"* (Prov. 20:11). Many churchgoers sing "Standing on the Promises" when all they are doing is sitting on the premises. **Too many people avoid discovering the secret of success because deep down they suspect the secret may be hard work.**

NUGGET #70

You Were Created To Be An Answer

The great basketball coach John Wooden said, "You cannot live a perfect day without doing something for someone who will never be able to repay you." A powerful scripture in the Bible that I believe releases the blessing of God in your life is Proverbs 3:27, which says, "*Withhold not good from them to whom it is due, when it is in the power of thine hand to do it.*" Joy shared is joy doubled. You were created to be a part of the solution. "I am only one, but still I am one. I cannot do everything, but still I can do something; I will not refuse to do the something I can do," said Helen Keller.

Be an answer. Get in the way if someone you know is on the way down. Walk in on someone you can help when others are walking out, because there are no unimportant jobs, no unimportant people, no unimportant acts of kindness. If you haven't got any kindness in your heart, you have the worst kind of heart trouble.

Your contribution is determined by the answers you give to the problems you face. According to Mike Murdock, "You will only be remembered for two things: the problems you solve or the ones you create." It's always more blessed to give than to receive (see Acts 20:35). Give of yourself to others, and watch criticism leave your life. Critics are usually the most inactive of people. Walk in your neighbor's shoes, sit in your boss's chair, run the path of your best friend. Be on the lookout for ways to be an answer.

How many happy selfish people do you know? You can make more friends in two months by helping other people than you can in two years by trying to get others to help you. **"The Dead Sea is a dead sea because it continually receives and never gives"** (Anonymous). *"If God can get it through you, God will give it to you,"* says Pastor E.V. Hill. Just one act of yours may be all it takes to turn the tide of another person's life.

NUGGET #71

Start With What You Have, Not What You Don't Have

God has already given you what you need to begin to create your future. Yet, most of us have found ourselves saying, "If only I had this...if only this were different...if only I had more money, then I could do what God wants me to do" all the while ignoring the seeds that God has planted within us. People always overstate the importance of things they don't have. **God will never ask you for something you can't give Him.** He wants you to start with what He has given you.

Don't let what you cannot do keep you from doing what you can do. Prolonged idleness paralyzes initiative. To the vacillating mind, everything is impossible because it seems so. Do not wait for extraordinary circumstances to do good; use ordinary situations. We don't need more strength, ability or greater opportunity. What we need is to use what we have.

"The lure of the distant and the difficult is deceptive. The great opportunity is where you are," said John Burroughs. **What you can do now is the only influence you have over your future.** No person can ever be happy until he has learned to enjoy what he has and not worry over what he does not have. True greatness consists of being great in little things. Don't grumble because you don't have what you want; be thankful you don't get what you deserve. "'We must do something' is the unanimous refrain. 'You begin' is the deadening reply," said Walter Dwight.

It is right to be content with what you have, never with what you are. Happiness will never come to those who fail to appreciate what they already have. **Most people make the mistake of looking too far ahead for things close by.**

You can never get much of anything done unless you go ahead and do it before you are ready. No one ever made a success of anything by first waiting until all the conditions were "just right." The Bible says in Ecclesiastes 11:4 TLB, "If you wait for perfect conditions, you will never get anything done." Everyone must row with the oars he has been given.

Don't waste time in doubts and fears about what you don't have; spend yourself in the task before you, knowing that the right performance of this hour's duties will be the best preparation for the years that follow it. "Grow where you are planted. Begin to weave, and God will give the thread" (German Proverb).

NUGGET #72

The One Who Leads The Parade Doesn't Drag His Feet

A leader has been defined as one who knows the way, goes the way and shows the way. A leader has a low tolerance for idleness. Idleness travels so slowly that poverty soon overtakes it. When a winner makes a mistake, he says, "I was wrong." When a loser makes a mistake, he says, "It wasn't my fault."

"You are only qualified to lead to the degree that you are willing to serve. If you are not willing to serve, you are not qualified to lead," says Edwin Louis Cole. Jesus said, "Whosoever will be great among you, let him be your minister; and whosoever will be chief among you, let him be your servant: Even as the Son of man came not to be ministered unto, but to minister" (Matt. 20:26-28).

To be mediocre is to drift; to be a leader is to steer. "The real leader has no need to lead — he is content to point the way," said Henry Miller. "Leadership is the capacity and will to rally men and women to a common purpose and character which inspires confidence," said Lord Montgomery. "Of a good leader, when his task is finished, his goal achieved, they will say, 'we did it ourselves,' " says Eleanor Doan.

General Eisenhower used to demonstrate the art of leadership with a simple piece of string. He'd put it on a table and say: "Pull it, and it'll follow wherever you wish. Push it, and it will go nowhere at all. It's the same way when it comes to leading people." A boss says, "Get going," a leader says, "Let's go." Be the leader you would want to be under.

NUGGET #73

Ten Truisms That Aren't True

1. The way to guarantee success is to work smarter, not harder.

This is a losing idea. You will find that effective leaders do both. They work smarter, and they work harder.

2. Activity equals accomplishment.

Activity is not accomplishment. Hard work is not results. We should not ask ourselves whether we're busy, but what we're busy about. We serve a God Who is interested in results.

3. Take care of things, and they will take care of you.

We should not take care, we should take control. If you don't take control of your own life, somebody else will.

4. If you want to be a success, you must pay the price.

You don't pay the price for success; you possess the price for success. The path to success belongs to you. It's not something that you have to give up in order to succeed.

5. Don't waste (kill) time.

Although this truism expresses a good thought, it is really not accurate. When you waste time, it is not time you are wasting, it is your very life.

6. If it's not broke, don't fix it.

That is not good advice. Even though things are working, many times they still can be significantly improved or modified.

7. What you see is what you get.

We Christians are commanded not to be moved by what we see but by the Word of God. We are to see the unseen in every situation of life.

8. He is a self-made man.

There is no such thing. A person can succeed only with the help of God and others.

9. Talk is cheap.

False. Talk is very expensive. What an individual says is ultimately what he gets — and what he pays for.

10. Practice makes perfect. No, perfect practice makes perfect. Wrong practice leads to wrong habits. Perfect practice leads to perfect action. Make sure that whatever you do on a regular basis is right and correct.

PART III:
LOOKING UPWARD

NUGGET #74

Stop Every Day And Look
At The Size Of God

Who is God? What is His personality like? What are His character traits?

According to the Bible, He is everlasting, just, caring, holy, divine, omniscient, omnipotent, omni-present and sovereign. He is light, perfection, abundance, salvation, wisdom, and love. He is the Creator, Savior, Deliverer, Redeemer, Provider, Healer, Advocate, and Friend. Never forget Who lives inside of you: *...the Lord...the great God, the great King above all gods* (Ps. 95:3 NIV).

John, the beloved disciple, tells us: *Ye are of God, little children, and have overcome them: because greater is he that is in you, than he that is in the world* (1 John 4:4). Period. Exclamation point. That settles it!

God and the devil are not equal, just opposite.

I travel by air quite often and one of the benefits is that every time I fly I get a glimpse of God's perspective. I like looking at my challenges from 37,000 feet in the air. **No problem is too large for God's intervention, and no person is too small for God's attention.**

God is always able. If you don't need miracles, you don't need God. Dave Bordon, a friend of mine, said it best: "I don't understand the situation, but I understand God."

The miraculous realm of God always has to do with multiplication, not addition.

God likens our life in Him to seedtime and harvest. Do you realize how miraculous that is? Let me give you a conservative example: Suppose one kernel of corn produces one stalk with two ears, each ear having 200 kernels. From those 400 kernels come 400 stalks with 160,000 kernels. All from one kernel planted only one season earlier.

Our confession to the Lord should be Jeremiah 32:17 (NIV): *"Ah, Sovereign Lord, you have made the heavens and the earth by your great power and outstretched arm. Nothing is too hard for you."*

God is bigger than _____ . Fill in the blank for your own life.

NUGGET #75

You Can Never See the Sunrise By Looking to the West

How you position yourself to receive makes all the difference. For example, as you read this book, if you position yourself to receive by saying to the Lord, "I will take action on what You show me," you will benefit more than if you read it just to be motivated or inspired. **Action springs not from thought, but from a readiness for responsibility.** Position yourself to be ready for responsibility.

I've known many people who were excellent reservoirs of learning yet never had an idea. "Eyes that look are common. Eyes that see are rare," says J. Oswald Sanders. **The problem is we're flooded with information and starving for revelation.**

To resist or receive is a choice we make every day. Nothing dies quicker than a new idea in a closed mind. It is impossible for a man to learn what he thinks he already knows. I believe that Jesus responded strongly to the Pharisees because they refused to position themselves to receive.

Availability is the greatest ability you have. The devil trembles when he hears God's weakest servant say, "Yes, Lord I'll do it!" When you're facing God, your back is turned to the devil. **Never give up control of your life to anything but faith.**

Our walk with God begins with the word "Follow" and ends with the word "Go!" Don't let success interfere with your relationship with God. The opportunities God sends won't wake up those who are asleep. "Kneeling is the proper posture for putting seeds into the ground," says Brooks Atkinson. **The Christian on his knees sees more than the world on its tiptoes.**

Opportunities can drop in your lap if you have your lap where opportunities drop. When you don't position yourself to receive, it's like praying for a bushel but only carrying a cup. Don't pray for rain if you're going to complain about the mud.

We typically see things, not as they are, but as we are. By how we position ourselves, we will see the evidence of God everywhere or nowhere. Too often our minds are locked on one track. We are looking for red, so we overlook blue; we are thinking tomorrow, and God is saying now; we are looking everywhere, and the answer is under our nose.

When a person is positioned correctly, he is ready to receive all that God has for him.

NUGGET #76

Face The Music, and Someday You Will Lead The Band

Not all obstacles are bad. In fact, an opportunity's favorite disguise is an obstacle. Conflict is simply meeting an obstacle on the road to your answer. The fight is good; it is proof that you haven't quit. The apostle Paul said it best when he wrote, "We are pressed on every side by troubles, but not crushed and broken. We are perplexed because we don't know why things happen as they do, but we don't give up and quit. We are hunted down, but God never abandons us. We get knocked down, but we get up again and keep going" (2 Cor. 4:8,9, TLB).

Being a Christian does not remove you from the world and its problems; rather, it equips you to live in it productively and victoriously. No one is immune to problems. Even the lion has to fight off flies. Growth and success don't eliminate obstacles; they create new ones. But God is always working on us and walking with us. Thomas Carlisle said, "The block of granite which was an obstacle in the pathway of the weak becomes a stepping-stone in the pathway of the strong."

Even in the midst of trials, God wants growth and promotion for you. Trials provide an opportunity to grow, not die. Obstacles can temporarily detour you, but only you can make you stop. **The devil wants you to think there's nothing more permanent than your temporary situation.** Obstacles reveal what we truly believe and who we really are. They introduce you to yourself. Your struggle may be lasting, but it is not everlasting.

As I've traveled, I've always noticed that no matter how cloudy it is when the plane takes off, above the clouds the sun always shines. Look up! It's not your outlook but your "uplook" that counts. Obstacles are a part of life. Jesus said, "In the world ye shall have tribulation: but be of good cheer; I have overcome the world" (John 16:33). Jesus does not say, "There is no storm." He says, "I am here; do not tremble, just trust." The difference between iron and steel is fire, but the fire-tried steel is worth it. God never promised that it would be easy. He did say "All things are possible to him that believeth" (Mark 9:23).

When God is at your side, He helps you face the music, even when you don't like the tune. **Don't just look to God through your circumstances; look at your circumstances through God.** "In the presence of trouble, some people grow wings; others buy crutches," said Harold W. Ruoff. If you want your place in the sun, you'll have to expect some blisters.

NUGGET #77

Fear Wants You to Run From Something That Isn't After You

The great evangelist Billy Sunday once said, "Fear knocked at my door. Faith answered...and there was no one there." Now, that's the proper response to fear. Why does fear like to take the place of faith? The two have a lot in common — both believe that what you cannot see will happen. Our worst imaginations almost never happen, and most worries die in vain anticipation. "It ain't no use putting up your umbrella till it rains," said Alice Caldwell Rice.

What you fear about tomorrow is not here yet. "Don't be afraid of the day you have never seen" (English Proverb). Fear holds you back from flexing your risk muscle. Faith ends where worry begins, and worry ends where faith begins. It's been said that worry is a darkroom where negatives are developed. Like a rocking chair, it keeps you going, but you don't get anywhere. A friend of mine once said, "Don't tell me that worry doesn't do any good. I know better. The things I worry about don't happen."

"The Lord is the strength of my life; of whom shall I be afraid?" (Ps. 27:1). "In God I trust; I will not be afraid. What can mortal man do to me?" (Ps. 56:4, NIV). **People would worry less about what others think of them if they only realized how seldom they do.** Most people believe their doubts and doubt their beliefs. So do like the old saying and "feed your faith and watch your doubts starve to death."

Many people are so filled with fear that they go through life running from something that isn't after them. Fear of the future is a waste of the present. **Fear not tomorrow. God is already there. Never be afraid to trust an unknown future to a known God.** If you can't help worrying, remember that worrying can't help you either.

Howard Chandler said, "Every morning I spend fifteen minutes filling my mind full of God; and there's no room left over for worry thoughts." A famous old poem in *The Prairie Pastor* said it best: "Said the robin to the sparrow, I should really like to know why these anxious human beings rush about and worry so. Said the sparrow to the robin, I think that it must be they have no Heavenly Father such as cares for you and me."

NUGGET #78

Ideas Go Away, But
Direction Stays

How do you know the difference between what comes to your mind, and direction from God? There is a persistency to direction. The Bible says in Proverbs 19:21 (NIV), *Many are the plans in a man's heart, but it is the Lord's purpose that prevails.* In Psalm 32:8 the Lord promises, *I will instruct thee and teach thee in the way which thou shalt go: I will guide thee with mine eye.*

When we know what God wants us to do, then we can have total confidence that what we are attempting is right and that God is on our side. Direction is simply this: a stream with banks. And the most far-reaching, challenging direction is the most significant, because God is in it.

Direction is a matter of fact; ideas are a matter of opinion. One characteristic of direction from God is that it will always be humanly impossible to follow and fulfill alone without Him.

Direction is the mother of divine discomfort. We should have a certain divine discomfort at all times. A sensing that God is always wanting to direct us every day. A stirring in our hearts so that we are never quite satisfied spiritually with where we are in God or what we're doing for Him. We believers should be known as a people with a mission, not people just fishin'. Evangelist R.W. Schambach puts it this way: "Be called and sent, not up and went." We are a people with a purpose, not a problem.

God always calls us to and from. In Colossians 1:12,13 the Apostle Paul writes:

Giving thanks unto the Father, which hath made us meet to be partakers of the inheritance of the saints in light:

Who hath delivered us from the power of darkness, and hath translated us into the kingdom of his dear Son.

Be sure to look for areas God is calling you out of as well as in to. There is also a difference between God's will in our lives and God's will for our lives. God's will for our lives are those things that He intends for every person — salvation, strength, health, peace, joy, etc. But God's will in our lives is unique to each individual. One person may be called to live in one place all his life, while another is called to move six times within ten years.

Never be afraid of the light of God's direction. Maurice Freehill said, "Who is more foolish, a child afraid of the dark or the man afraid of the light?" Know this: wherever God guides, He provides. And where God calls, He appoints and anoints to do the work. Lay hold of those persistent directions in your life, and tap into the power of God's will for you.

NUGGET #79

Retreat To Advance

Sometimes the most important and urgent thing we can do is get away to a peaceful and anointed spot.

This is one of the most powerful concepts that I personally have incorporated into my life. I'm sitting right now writing this book in a cabin up on a hill overlooking a beautiful lake, miles away from the nearest city.

As we choose to draw away for a time, we can see and hear much more clearly about how to go ahead. Jesus did this many times during His earthly life, especially just before and after major decisions. The Bible says, ...*in quietness and in confidence shall be your strength*...(Is. 30:15). There's something invigorating and renewing about retreating to a quiet place of rest and peace. Silence is an environment in which great ideas are birthed.

There really are times when you should not see people, times when you should direct your whole attention toward God. I believe that every person should have a place of refuge, one out of the normal scope of living, one where he can "retreat to advance" and "focus in" with just the Lord and himself.

It is important to associate intently and as often as possible with your loftiest dreams. In Isaiah 40:31 we read, *But they that wait upon the Lord shall renew their strength; they shall*

mount up with wings as eagles; they shall run, and not be weary; and they shall walk, and not faint. Learn to wait upon the Lord.

Make a regular appointment with yourself; it will be one of the most important you can ever have during the course of a week or a month. Choose to retreat to advance. See how much clearer you move forward with God as a result.

NUGGET #80

It Is As Important To Know What God Can't Do As To Know What He Can Do

1. God cannot lie.

2. God cannot change.

3. God cannot recall our sins after we've asked for forgiveness.

4. God cannot be the author of confusion.

5. God cannot leave us or forsake us.

6. God cannot go back on His promises.

7. God cannot revoke His gifts.

8. God cannot be pleased without faith.

9. God cannot be defeated.

10. God cannot be too big for our problems.

11. God cannot be too little for our problems.

12. God cannot prefer one person over another.

13. God cannot break His covenant.

14. God cannot revoke His calling.

15. God cannot be unjust.

16. God cannot do anything contrary to the Scriptures.

17. God cannot bless a lie.

18. God cannot love sin.

19. God cannot give anything to a double-minded man.

20. God cannot be forced into an impossible situation.

21. God cannot ignore the praises of His people.

22. God cannot be our problem.

23. God cannot be overcome by the world.

24. God cannot be late.

25. God cannot be neutral.

26. God cannot be weak.

27. God cannot bless doubt.

28. God cannot withhold wisdom from those who ask in faith.

29. God cannot be against us.

30. God cannot be limited or confined.

NUGGET #81

Expect The Opposite

One of the major reasons the Bible was written was to teach us to expect the opposite of what we see in the world. Indeed, **"I can't believe my eyes" is a very spiritual statement, for we are called to walk by faith and not by sight.** One of God's principles of opposites is found in John 3:30: "He [Jesus] must increase, but I must decrease." God tells us we must give to receive, die to live and serve to lead. In this world of opposites — what Pat Robertson calls "the upside-down kingdom" — "He who goes to and fro weeping...shall indeed come again with a shout of joy" (Ps. 126:6, NAS), and "He that loseth his life for my [Jesus'] sake shall find it" (Matt 10:39).

When fear comes, expect the opposite — faith to rise up inside you.

When symptoms attack your body, expect the opposite — God's healing power to touch you.

When sadness tries to attach itself to you, expect the opposite — joy to flood your being.

When lack comes in, expect the opposite — God's provision to meet your needs.

When confusion comes, expect the opposite — God's peace to comfort you.

When darkness tries to cover you, expect the opposite — God's light to shine on you.

God chooses ordinary men and women for extraordinary work. "Ye see your calling, brethren, how that not many wise men after the flesh, not many mighty, not many noble, are called: But God hath chosen the foolish things of the world to confound the wise; and God hath chosen the weak things of the world to confound the things which are mighty...that no flesh should glory in his presence" (1 Cor. 1:26,27,29).

In the midst of your destiny, if you feel unwise and weak, fret not. God is getting ready to move on your behalf. **The Sermon on the Mount was preached to lift us out of the Valley of Discouragement.** If you want to go higher, go deeper.

This famous poem said it best:

Doubt sees the obstacles
Faith sees the way.
Doubt sees the darkest night
Faith sees the day.
Doubt dreads to take a step
Faith soars on high.
Doubt questions "who believes?"
Faith answers "I."

—Anonymous

NUGGET #82

Don't Miss the Silver Lining Only Looking for The Gold

Jesus never taught men how to make a living. He taught men how to live. "God doesn't call us to be successful. He calls us to be faithful," said Albert Hubbard. Most people have their eye on the wrong goal. Is more money, a higher position or more influence your goal? These are not true goals, but rather simply by-products of goals.

What is a true goal? It is this: "Do not let this Book of the Law depart from your mouth; meditate on it day and night, so that you may be careful to do everything written in it. Then you will be prosperous and successful" (Josh. 1:8, NIV). We should work to become, not to acquire.

Seek not success. Instead, seek the truth, and you will find both. "But seek ye first the kingdom of God, and his righteousness; and all these things shall be added unto you" (Matt. 6:33).

"Happiness is not a reward — it is a consequence. Suffering is not a punishment — it is a result," said Robert Green Ingersoll. Do the very best you can, and leave the results to God. **Potential is the most empty word in the world, but with God it can be filled to overflowing.**

How small a portion of earth will keep us when we are dead, we who ambitiously seek after the whole world while we are living! "And how does a man benefit if he gains the whole world and loses his soul in the process?" (Mark 8:36, TLB). People are funny; they spend money they don't have, to buy things they don't need, to impress people they don't like.

Success lies, not in achieving what you aim at, but in aiming at what you ought to achieve. Do what God wants you to do, and He will take care of the rest.

NUGGET #83

Have A Ready Will And Walk, Not Idle Time And Talk

Acting on God's will is like riding a bicycle: if you don't go on, you go off!

Once we know God's will and timing, we should be instant to obey, taking action without delay. Delay and hesitation when God is telling us to do something now is sin. The longer we take to act on whatever God wants us to do, the more unclear His directives become. We need to make sure that we are on God's interstate highway and not in a cul-de-sac.

Ours is a God of velocity. He is a God of timing and direction. These two always go together. It is never wise to act upon only one or the other. Jumping at the first opportunity seldom leads to a happy landing. In Proverbs 25:8 the writer tells us, *Go not forth hastily to strive, lest thou know not what to do in the end thereof, when thy neighbour hath put thee to shame.* A famous saying holds that people can be divided into three groups: 1) those who make things happen, 2) those who watch things happen, and 3) those who wonder what's happening. Even the right direction taken at the wrong time is a bad decision.

Most people miss out on God's best in their lives because they're not prepared. The Bible warns us that we should be prepared continually. The Apostle Paul exhorts us: *...be instant in season, out of season...*(2 Tim. 4:2).

189

There is a seasonality to God. In Ecclesiastes 3:1 we read: *To every thing there is a season, and a time to every purpose under heaven.* Everything that you and I are involved in will have a spring (a time of planting and nurturing), a summer (a time of greatest growth), a fall (a time of harvest), and a winter (a time of decisions and planning).

Relax. Perceive, understand, and accept God's divine timing and direction.

NUGGET #84

Don't Spend Your Life Standing at the Complaint Counter

The person who is always finding fault seldom finds anything else. Live your life as an exclamation, not an explanation. **Any complainer will tell you success is nothing but luck.** Children are born optimists, and the world slowly tries to educate them out of their "delusion." The fact is, the more you complain the less you'll obtain. A life of complaining is the ultimate rut. The only difference between a rut and a grave is the timing. A complaining spirit is first a caller, then a guest and finally a master.

Some people always find the bad in a situation. Do you know people like that? How many successful complainers do you know? "Little men with little minds and little imagination go through life in little ruts, smugly resisting all changes which would jar their little worlds" (Anonymous). Small things affect small minds. Some people are confident they could move mountains if only someone else would just clear the rocks out of their way. **Some of the most disappointed people in the world are those who get what is coming to them.**

When you feel like complaining, bring God into the situation. You have to shut out His light to be in the dark. "Thou wilt keep him in perfect peace, whose mind is stayed on thee" (Is. 26:3). Are you waiting on God, or is He waiting on you? Is God your hope or your excuse? Don't let heaven become only a complaint counter.

"Of all sad words of tongue or pen, the saddest are these: 'It might have been!'" (John Greenleaf Whittier). Don't complain. **The wheel that squeaks the loudest often gets replaced.** If you complain about other people, you have no time to love them.

NUGGET #85

The Sky's Not The Limit

No one can put a limit on you without your permission.

"Eli Whitney was laughed at when he showed his cotton gin. Edison had to install his electric light free of charge in an office building before anyone would even look at it. The first sewing machine was smashed to pieces by a Boston mob. People scoffed at the idea of railroads. People thought that traveling thirty miles an hour would stop the circulation of the blood. Morse had to plead before ten Congresses before they would even look at his telegraph" (Anonymous). Yet, for all these men the sky was not the limit. Beware of those who stand aloof and greet each venture with reproof; the world would stop if things were run by men who say, "It can't be done."

"Seek, and ye shall find" (Matt. 7:7). We attain only in proportion to what we attempt. **More people are persuaded into believing in nothing than believing too much.** Jesus said, "According to your faith be it unto you" (Matt. 9:29). You are never as far from the answer as it first appears. It's never safe or accurate to look into the future without faith.

Tell me what you believe about Jesus, and I will tell you some important facts about your future. What picture of Jesus do you have? You should be more concerned about what the still small voice whispers than about what other people shout.

A lot of people no longer hope for the best, they just hope to avoid the worst. Many of us have heard opportunity knocking at our door, but by the time we unhooked the chain, pushed back the bolt, turned two locks and shut off the burglar alarm — it was gone! Too many people spend their lives looking around, looking down or looking behind, when God says to look up. The sky's not the limit!

NUGGET #86

God Made You. . .

God made you different, not indifferent.

God made you extraordinary, not ordinary.

God made you significant, not insignificant.

God made you attached, not detached.

God made you competent, not incompetent.

God made you compatible, not incompatible.

God made you active, not inactive.

God made you indispensable, not dispensable.

God made you effective, not defective.

God made you adept, not inept.

God made you distinct, not indistinct.

God made you adequate, not inadequate.

God made you efficient, not inefficient.

God made you superior, not inferior.

God made you responsible, not irresponsible.

God made you solvent, not insolvent.

God made you sane, not insane.

God made you efficient, not deficient.

God made you consistent, not inconsistent.

God made you insightful, not despiteful.

God made you irresistible, not resistible.

God made you sensitive, not insensitive.

God made you uncommon, not common.

God made you decisive, not indecisive.

God made you an original, not a copy.

NUGGET #87

Believe Six Impossible
Things Before Breakfast

Imagine beginning tomorrow as you have never done before. Instead of just stretching your body when you get out of bed, stretch your very being with all of the good things God has in store for you. Think, plan, believe and pray for things that require God's involvement. Gain control of your day.

Grab hold of each day from the start. Most people lose an hour at the beginning of the day and spend the rest of the day trying to recapture it. **The first hour of the morning is the rudder of the day.** Never begin your day in neutral. Take the offensive — never meet trouble halfway. Create a habit of initiative. It's the person who doesn't need a boss who's usually selected to be one. When you're a self-starter, others don't have to be a crank.

Duties delayed are the devil's delight. The devil doesn't care what your plans are as long as you don't do anything about them. **You will never gain what you are unwilling to go after.** The key to your future is hidden in your daily approach to life.

Seize your destiny. Don't let it slip away. **"If God has called you, don't look over your shoulder to see who is following you"** (Anonymous). "Let every man abide in the same calling wherein he was called" (1 Cor. 7:20). "The crude

197

and physical agony of the cross was nothing compared to the indifference of the crowd on Main Street as Jesus passed by," said Allan Knight Chalmers.

Satan trembles when he sees the weakest Christian taking the offensive. "The breakfast of Christian champions is early morning prayer," says Billy Joe Daugherty. God is worth your time. Don't begin your day in reverse.

NUGGET #88

God's Call Is Heard, Not Seen

Just because an opportunity presents itself for which we are qualified does not necessarily mean that it is God's will for us to accept it. Many times circumstances "line up" and everything looks good, yet it doesn't seem right. In such cases, we need to hear from God. That's why I say that divine direction is really heard and not seen. We Christians should be more interested in the unseen than we are in the things that are visible.

The only safe way to decide which direction to go is by learning to distinguish between the voices we hear. There are always three sources of voices: there's God's voice, our own voice, and the devil's voice. We must learn to distinguish among these three.

We must choose to eliminate all foggy areas in our lives. This is the key to being able to see and think clearly. Fog is very dangerous to drive into, especially a spiritual fog.

We believers should choose to build on what we hear on the inside, not what we see on the outside. There's a big difference between having an ability to do something, and being called and anointed to do it. As you have sat in church, you may have seen someone who has an ability to sing, but that is not necessarily evidence that the person has been called of God to the life of a singer. A gift is not a call.

I am not suggesting that when we have the ability to do something that God isn't directing us to use that ability. But ability should not be the only criterion for deciding whether or not we make a particular choice. Not only does the Lord give us a road map, He also provides direction signals, information signs, a vehicle, fuel, and time to get to our destination.

We need to be sensitive to what lies in the unseen. Many people have walked right over rich pools of oil or veins of gold, not realizing what lay just beneath their feet. Their vision was too limited. They only saw the ground, not the treasure hidden in it.

Look beyond what you see with your natural eyes. Listen with your spiritual ears. Keep your antenna up for God's perfect direction in your life.

NUGGET #89

What Good Is Aim If You Never Pull The Trigger?

God is a God of timing and direction. He wants us to know what to do and when to do it. Psalm 32:8 says, "I will instruct thee and teach thee in the way which thou shalt go: I will guide thee with mine eye." Don't live your life ahead of God's will or outside of His will.

Patience will do wonders, but it was not much help to the man who planted an orange grove in Alaska. There is never a right time to do the wrong thing. **If you take too long in deciding what to do with your life, you'll find you've lived it.** Time was invented by Almighty God in order to give dreams a chance. "Hell is truth seen too late — duty neglected in its season," says Tyron Edwards. Ideas won't keep. Something must be done about them. "There is one thing stronger than all the armies in the world, and that is an idea whose time has come," says Victor Hugo.

Always apply light and not heat to your dreams. God says His "word is a lamp unto my feet, and a light unto my path" (Ps. 119:105). The lamp illuminates things we are dealing with now. The light directs our future. Jumping to a wrong decision seldom leads to a happy landing. Too many people leave the right opportunity to look for other opportunities. Seize today's opportunities today and tomorrow's opportunities tomorrow. Don't hurry when success depends on accuracy. Those who make the worst use of their time are the first to complain of its shortness. The fastest running back is useless unless heading toward the right goal line.

Timing is the vital ingredient for success. "For the vision is yet for an appointed time" (Hab. 2:3). There is an appointed time for your vision. Have 20/20 vision, don't be too far-sighted or too near-sighted. As I've studied godly leaders, I have found that at key times they have said, "God led me to do...."

Following His will releases the originality within you and helps you identify priorities. If Jesus is the Way, why waste time traveling some other way?

NUGGET #90

Is God Finished With You Yet?

If you are still breathing, the answer is no. Don't die until you're dead. Psalm 138:8 says, "The Lord will perfect that which concerneth me." God is continually perfecting and fine-tuning each of us. He wants to fulfill all of His promises and purposes in our lives.

"The creation of a thousand forests is in one acorn," said Ralph Waldo Emerson. The creation of your destiny is held within the seeds of your God-given ideas.

God begins with a positive and ends with a positive. "Being confident of this, that he who began a good work in you will carry it on to completion until the day of Christ Jesus" (Phil. 1:6, NIV). Jesus hasn't come back, so that means God isn't finished with you. God's will for us is momemtum, building from one good work to another.

Don't just go on to other things, go on to higher things. The pains of being a Christian are all growing pains, and those growing pains lead to maturity. God's way becomes plain as we walk in it. When faith is stretched, it grows. "The more we do the more we can do," said William Hazlitt.

Greater opportunity and momentum are the rewards of past accomplishment. **Success makes failures out of too many people when they stop after a victory.** When we do what we can, God will do what we can't. He's not finished!

NUGGET #91

It Is More Valuable To Seek God's Presence Than To Seek His Presents

The Bible presents four benefits of seeking God's presence.

The first benefit is joy. In Psalm 16:11 (NIV), the psalmist says of the Lord, *You have made known to me that path of life; you will fill me with joy in your presence, with eternal pleasures at your right hand.* We cannot help but experience great joy in our lives when we are in the presence of the Lord.

A second benefit of seeking God's presence is that it provides great light. In Psalm 89:15 (NIV) we read, *Blessed are those who have learned to acclaim you, who walk in the light of your presence, O Lord.* Wherever God is, there is great illumination. If there is a dark area in your life, an area in which you are having difficulty seeing, invite the presence of the Lord into that area. If you are having problems with your work, invite the presence of God on the job with you. If you are having difficulty at home, invite the presence of the Lord into your home. The mere presence of God will bring illumination and cause all darkness to leave. It will shed great light on your path.

A third benefit of seeking His presence is God's divine protection. Psalm 31:20 (NIV) says, *In the shelter of your presence you hide them from the intrigues of men; in your*

dwelling you keep them safe from the strife of tongues. Thank God for His divine protection and shelter in our lives. Everyone needs a hiding place, a place of safety and refuge. The presence of God provides a shelter to keep us from men and their vain words against us. If you're troubled by other people and by what they are saying, invite God's presence into those circumstances. If you work in a negative atmosphere, one in which what men are saying or doing is creating problems for you, invite the presence of God into that situation. He will be a shelter, a hiding place for you.

The fourth benefit of seeking God's presence is found in 1 John 3:19 (NIV): *This then is how we know that we belong to the truth, and how we set our hearts at rest in his presence.* There is great peace and great rest in the presence of God. Trouble, nervousness, anxiety, unrest, all these flee from the presence of the Lord.

Invite God's presence wherever you are. He will encamp around about you every minute and be with you in every situation of life. In His presence you will find great joy and light, divine protection, peace, and rest.

NUGGET #92

When Wisdom Reigns, It Pours

We should expect wisdom to be given to us. The Bible says in James 1:5, *If any of you lack wisdom, let him ask of God, that giveth to all men liberally, and upbraideth not; and it shall be given him.*

When you have heard God's voice, you have heard His wisdom. Thank God for His powerful wisdom. It forces a passage through the strongest barriers.

Wisdom is seeing everything from God's perspective. It is knowing when and how to use the knowledge that comes from the Lord. The old saying is true, "He who knows nothing, doubts nothing." But it is also true that he who knows has a solid basis for his belief.

Just think, we human beings have available to us the wisdom of the Creator of the universe. Yet **so few drink at the fountain of His wisdom; most just rinse out their mouths.** Many may try to live without the wisdom of the bread of life, but they will die in their efforts.

The world doesn't spend billions of dollars for wisdom. It spends billions in search of wisdom. Yet it is readily available to everyone who seeks its divine source.

There are ten steps to gaining godly wisdom:

1. Fear God (Ps. 111:10)

2. Please God (Eccl. 2:26)

3. Hear God (Prov. 2:6)

4. Look to God (Prov. 3:13)

5. Choose God's way (Prov. 8:10,11)

6. Be humble before God (Prov. 11:2)

7. Take God's advice (Prov. 13:10)

8. Receive God's correction (Prov. 29:15)

9. Pray to God (Eph. 1:17)

10. Know the Son of God (1 Cor. 1:30)

NUGGET #93

We Stand Tallest When We Are On Our Knees

The strongest action that you can take in any situation is to go to your knees and ask God for help. Whatever is worth worrying about is certainly worth praying about. Prayer unlocks God's treasure chest of great ideas.

I will share with you one of my favorite prayers. It is one word: help.

"Help, help, help!"

When we pray, we must be simultaneously willing to take the action that God directs in answer to our prayer.

There are four levels of prayer:

Level #1 is petition: "Father, I need...."

Level #2 is intercession: "God, help...."

Level #3 is praise and thanksgiving: "Thanks, Lord!"

Level #4 is conversation: "Good morning, Father."

In Philippians 4:6,7 (NIV) the Apostle Paul counsels us, *Do not be anxious about anything, but in everything, by*

prayer and petition, with thanksgiving, present your requests to God. And the peace of God, which transcends all understanding, will guard your hearts and your minds in Christ Jesus. In Colossians 4:2 (NIV) he says, *Devote yourselves to prayer, being watchful and thankful.*

There are twelve benefits to prayer:

1. Prayer defeats the devil. (Matt. 18:18)

2. Prayer saves the unbeliever. (Acts 2:21)

3. Prayer edifies the believer. (Jude 20)

4. Prayer sends laborers into the harvest. (Matt. 9:38)

5. Prayer heals the sick. (James 5:13-15)

6. Prayer overcomes the impossible. (Matt. 21:22)

7. Prayer changes the natural. (James 5:17,18)

8. Prayer brings the right things to pass. (Matt. 7:7-11)

9. Prayer imparts wisdom. (James 1:5)

10. Prayer brings peace. (Phil. 4:5-7)

11. Prayer guards against temptation. (Matt. 26:41)

12. Prayer reveals God's answers. (Luke 11:9,10)

NUGGET #94

Adopt The Pace of God

God is a planner, a strategist. He is incredibly organized and has a definite pace. More like a marathon runner than a sprinter, He has our whole lives in mind, not just tomorrow. Never try to hurry God. "He that believeth shall not make haste," the Bible says in Isaiah 28:16. Pressure usually accompanies us when we are out of the pace of God.

Proverbs 16:9 (TLB) says, "We should make plans — counting on God to direct us." Proverbs 16:3 (NIV) tells us, "Commit to the Lord whatever you do, and your plans will succeed." Cowards never start, and the lukewarm die along the way. **God is the original's hope and the copy's excuse. Is God your hope or your excuse?**

Adopt the pace of God; His secret is patience. There is no time lost in waiting if you are waiting on the Lord. **All great achievements require time.** Happiness is a direction, not a destination.

Abraham Lincoln, during the darkest hours of the Civil War, said in response to the question whether he was sure God was on his side, "I do not know: I have not thought about that. But I am very anxious to know whether we are on God's side." Urgent matters are seldom urgent. "The strength of a man consists in finding out the way God is going, and going that way," said Henry Ward Beecher.

Walking in the pace of God helps establish us on the proper foundation. Nothing is permanent unless it is built on

God's will and God's Word. "Except the Lord build the house, they labour in vain that build it" (Ps. 127:1). "The steps of a good man are ordered by the Lord: and he delighteth in his way" (Ps. 37:23). Never remain where God has not sent you. **A Christian with the right pace is like a candle, which must keep cool and burn at the same time.** But if you burn the candle at both ends, you are not as bright as you think.

Every great person first learned how to obey, whom to obey and when to obey. The road to success runs uphill, so don't expect to break any speed records. A famous anonymous poem says, "The place I choose, or place I shun, my soul is satisfied with none; but when Thy will directs my way, 'tis equal joy to go or stay."

NUGGET #95

Hearing Tells You That The Music Is Playing; Listening Tells You What The Song Is Saying

---

One of the least developed skills among us human beings is that of listening. There are really two different kinds of listening. There is the natural listening in interaction with other people, and there is spiritual listening to the voice of God.

It has been said, "Men are born with two ears, but only one tongue, which indicates that they were meant to listen twice as much as they talk." In natural communication, leaders always "monopolize the listening." **What we learn about another person will always result in a greater reward than what we tell him about ourselves.** We need to learn to listen and observe aggressively. We must try harder to truly listen, and not just to hear.

In regard to spiritual listening, Proverbs 8:34,35 (NIV) quotes wisdom who says:

Blessed is the man who listens to me, watching daily at my doors, waiting at my doorway.

For whoever finds me finds life and receives favor from the Lord.

There is great wisdom and favor to be gained by listening.

Proverbs 15:31 (NIV) says, *He who listens to a life-giving rebuke will be at home among the wise.* Listening allows us to maintain a teachable spirit. It increases our "teach-ability." Those who give us a life-giving rebuke can be a great blessing to us.

The Bible teaches that we are to be quick to listen and slow to speak. (James 1:19.) We must never listen passively, especially to God. If we resist hearing, a hardening can take place in our lives. Callousness can develop. In Luke 16:31 (NIV), Jesus said of a certain group of people, "...`If they do not listen to Moses and the Prophets, they will not be convinced even if someone rises from the dead.`" The more we resist listening to the voice of God, the more hardened and less fine-tuned our hearing becomes.

There are results of spiritual hearing, as we see in Luke 8:15 (NIV). This passage relates to the parable of the sower: "*...the seed on good soil stands for those with a noble and good heart, who hear the word, retain it, and by persevering produce a crop.*" Harvest is associated not only with persevering and good seed in good soil, but also with those people who hear the Word of God and retain it.

Fine-tune your natural and spiritual ears to listen and learn.

NUGGET #96

Focus Changes Everything

First Corinthians 9:25 (TLB) says, "To win the contest you must deny yourselves many things that would keep you from doing your best." Doing too many things always keeps you from doing your best. **One surefire way to bring focus into your life is never to place a question mark where God has put a period.**

One man with focus constitutes a majority. The person who begins too much accomplishes too little. If you wait to do a great deal of good at once, you will never do anything. He that is everywhere is really nowhere. "Better is a handful with quietness, than both the hands full with travail and vexation of spirit" (Eccl. 4:6). When you don't have a good reason for doing a thing, you have one good reason for letting it alone. **It's amazing the amount of work you can get done if you don't do anything else.**

"Every human mind is a great slumbering power until awakened by a keen, specific desire and by definite resolution to do," says Edgar F. Roberts. Focus is one of the most necessary ingredients of character, and one of the best instruments of success. Without focus, creativity wastes its efforts in a maze of inconsistencies.

Few things are impossible to diligence and focus. **Whatever you focus your attention upon you give strength and momentum to.** Focus is the secret of strength. When you please everyone, you please no one. To be everywhere is to be nowhere.

Jesus said in Luke 14:33, "Whosoever he be of you that forsaketh not all that he hath, he cannot be my disciple." Being a disciple of Christ requires focus. When you walk in focus, you'll become passionate about your dream; you'll find it expressed everywhere — you can even smell it. You can't do everything, but you can do something.

The straight and narrow way has the lowest accident rate. It is important that people know what you stand for; it is equally important that they know what you won't stand for. We cannot do everything we want to do, but we can do everything God wants us to do.

NUGGET #97

God Is Not Your Problem; God Is On Your Side

Some time ago I was eating at a Mexican fast food restaurant. As I stood in line for service I noticed in front of me a very poor elderly lady who looked like a street person. When it came her turn, she ordered some water and one taco. As I sat in the booth right next to her, I couldn't help but observe and be moved with compassion toward her. Shortly after I had begun my meal I went over to her and asked if I could buy some more food for her lunch. She looked at me and angrily asked, "Who are you?"

"Just a guy who wants to help you," I responded. She ignored me. I finished my meal about the same time she did, and we both got up to leave. I felt led to give her some money. In the parking lot I approached her and offered her some cash. Her only response to me was, "Stop bothering me." Then, she stormed off.

Immediately, the Lord showed me that this is often the way many of us respond to Him. When He calls out to us, seeking to bless us, we act as though we don't even know Who He is. We respond to His offer of blessing by asking," Who are You? What do You want from me?" The Lord, being the gracious God He is, continues to try to bless us. Yet we react by saying, "Stop bothering me."We walk off, just as this lady did, missing out on the rich blessings of the Lord.

It's not the absence of problems that gives us peace; it's God's presence with us in the problems. In Matthew 28:20, Jesus sent His disciples into all the world, ordering them to preach the Gospel to every creature: *Teaching them to observe all things whatsoever I have commanded you; and, lo, I am with you alway, even unto the end of the world.* In Romans 8:38,39 (NIV), the Apostle Paul writes, *For I am convinced that neither death nor life, neither angels nor demons, neither the present nor the future, nor any powers, neither height nor depth, nor anything else in all creation, will be able to separate us from the love of God that is in Christ Jesus our Lord.* In verse 31 he declares, *What, then, shall we say in response to this? If God is for us, who can be against us?* A paraphrase might be, "If God is for us, who cares who is against us?"

In Psalm 145:18 (NIV), we read, *The Lord is near to all who call on him, to all who call on him in truth.* James 4:8 (NIV) admonishes us, *Come near to God and he will come near to you.* In Acts 17:27 (NIV) Paul speaks: "`For in him we live and move and have our being.'"

Thank God that we can, without hesitation and with full confidence, lean on His eternal faithfulness.

NUGGET #98

Learn The Alphabet
For Success

A Action

B Belief

C Commitment

D Direction

E Enthusiasm

F Faith

G Goals

H Happiness

I Inspiration

J Judgment

K Knowledge

L Love

M Motivation

N Nonconformity

O Obedience

P Persistence

Q Quality

R Righteousness

S Steadfastness

T Thankfulness

U Uniqueness

V Vision

W Wisdom

X (E)xcellence

Y Yieldedness

Z Zeal

NUGGET #99

God Will Use You Right Where You Are Today

You don't need to do anything else for God to begin to use you now. You don't have to read another paperback book, listen to another cassette tape, memorize another scripture, plant another seed gift, or repeat another creed or confession. You don't even need to attend another church service before God will begin to make use of you.

God uses willing vessels, not brimming vessels. Throughout the Bible, in order to fulfill His plans for the earth, God used many people from all walks of life. He used:

1. Matthew, a government employee, who became an apostle.

2. Gideon, a common laborer, who became a valiant leader of men.

3. Jacob, a deceiver, whose name became Israel.

4. Deborah, a housewife, who became a judge.

5 Moses, a stutterer, who became a deliverer.

6. Jeremiah, a child, who fearlessly spoke the Word of the Lord.

7. Aaron, a servant, who became God's spokesman.

8. Nicodemus, a Pharisee, who became a defender of the faith.

9. David, a shepherd boy, who became a king.

10. Hosea, a marital failure, who prophesied to save Israel.

11. Joseph, a prisoner, who became prime minister.

12. Esther, an orphan, who became a queen.

13. Elijah, a homely man, who became a mighty prophet.

14. Joshua, an assistant, who became a conqueror.

15. James and John, fishermen, who became close disciples of Christ and were known as "sons of thunder."

16. Abraham, a nomad, who became the father of many nations.

17. Jacob, a refugee, who became the father of the twelve tribes of Israel.

18. John the Baptist, a vagabond, who became the fore runner of Jesus.

19. Mary, an unknown virgin, who gave birth to the Son of God.

20. Nehemiah, a cupbearer, who built the wall of Jerusalem.

21. Shadrach, Meshach, and Abednego, Hebrew exiles, who became great leaders of the nation of Babylon.

22. Hezekiah, a son of an idolatrous father, who became a king renowned for doing right in the sight of the Lord.

23. Isaiah, a man of unclean lips, who prophesied the birth of God's Messiah.

24. Paul, a persecutor, who became the greatest mis sionary in history and author of two-thirds of the New Testament.

All God needs to use you is all of you!

NUGGET #100

Something Dominates Everyone's Day

What influence dominates your day? Is it the daily news, your negative neighbor, the memory of a failure? Or is it God's plan for you, His Word in your heart, a song of praise to Him? **Let the plan that God has for your life dominate your day, or something else will.**

An original knows what to fight for and what to compromise on. A copy compromises on what he shouldn't and fights for what isn't worth fighting for. Mediocrity has its own type of intensity. It can influence and affect every area of your life if you let it.

A fruitful life is not the result of chance. Faith honors God; God honors faith. There are a thousand ways of pleasing God, but not one without faith. "Some temptations come to the industrious, but all temptations attack the idle" (Spurgeon). God still speaks to those who take the time to listen. **There are no shortcuts to any destination worth reaching.**

Small mounds of dirt add up to a mountain. If you are not alert to pray, the mountain can dominate your day. It only takes the faith of a mustard seed to start the day over obstacle-free. If you wake up on the wrong side of the bed, roll off, kneel and pray to God instead.

A FINAL WORD

Be the whole person God called you to be. Don't settle for anything less. Don't look back. Look forward and decide today to take steps toward His plan for your life.

And remember First Thessalonians 5:24: *Faithful is he that calleth you, who also will do it.*

Additional copies of
An Enemy Called Average
are available from your local bookstore,
or directly from:

Insight International
P.O. Box 162002
Altamonte Springs, FL 32716-2002

(Volume discounts available)

John Mason welcomes the opportunity to minister to your church, in conferences, retreats, or in men's, women's, and youth groups.

Available from Insight International are the following inspiring videos:

Momentum: How To Get it, How To Have It, How To Keep It.

The Good Things About Bad Things.

Don't Quit.

Books Available:

An Enemy Called Average (paperback)

You're Born An Original — Don't Die A Copy (paperback)

Also available is the following tape series:

An Enemy Called Average

You're Born An Original — Don't Die A Copy

Send all prayer requests and inquiries to:

John Mason
Insight International
P.O. Box 162002
Altamonte Springs, FL 32716-2002

John Mason is the founder and president of Insight International, a ministry dedicated to bringing excellence and efficiency to Christian ministries and businesses. Several hundred businesses and ministries throughout the United States and abroad have benefitted from his counsel. John Mason's ministry exhorts believers to exercise all their gifts and talents while fulfilling God's whole plan for their lives. He is the author of several leadership manuals and tape series. He holds a Bachelor of Science degree in Business Administration from Oral Roberts University.

He also has the call and a powerful anointing to preach and minister to churches, men's and women's organizations and other Christian groups.

John was blessed to be raised in a Christian home in Fort Wayne, Indiana, by his parents Chet and Lorene Mason. He, his wife Linda and their four children Michelle, Greg, Mike, and David currently reside in Orlando, Florida.

Recommended Reading List

1. *The Bible* (Various Publishers)
2. *You and You Network* — Fred Smith (Word Publishing)
3. *See You At the Top* — Zig Ziglar (Pelican Publishing Co.)
4. *Stay in the Game* — Van Crouch (Honor Books)
5. *Maximized Manhood* — Edwin Louis Cole (Whitaker House Publishers)
6. *University of Success* — Og Mandino (Bantam Books)
7. *The One-Minute Businessman's/Businesswoman's Devotional* — Mike Murdock (Honor Books)
8. *I Dare You* — William Danforth (American Youth Foundation)
9. *How To Win Friends and Influence People* — Dale Carnegie (Simon and Schuster)
10. *Life Is Tremendous* — Charlie Jones (Tyndale House Publishers)
11. *The Greatest Salesman in the World* — Og Mandino (Bantam Books)
12. *Mary Kay on People Management* — Mary Kay Ash (Warner Books)
13. *Seven Habits of Highly Effective People* — Stephen R. Covey (Simon and Schuster)
14. *The One-Minute Manager* — Kenneth Blanchard (William Morrow & Co.)
15. *Rhinoceros Success* — Scott Alexander (The Rhino's Press)

NOTES

NOTES

NOTES

NOTES

NOTES

NOTES